UNDER THE RECEDING WAVE

Other works by C. P. Curran:

Dublin Decorative Plasterwork of the 17th and 18th Centuries, London 1967.

James Joyce Remembered. London 1968.

UNDER THE RECEDING
WAVE

C. P. CURRAN

Period photographs specially prepared by George Morrison

GILL AND MACMILLAN

Published by

GILL AND MACMILLAN LTD

2 Belvedere Place

Dublin 1

and in London through association with

MACMILLAN AND CO LTD

Cover design by Des Fitzgerald

Printed and bound in the Republic of Ireland by
Cahill and Co Limited

To my daughter

ELIZABETH

Though the great song return no more
There's keen delight in what we have:
The rattle of pebbles on the shore
Under the receding wave.

The Nineteenth Century and After
W. B. Yeats.

Contents

Chapter

Illustrations

1   *A Townscape with Figures*

M<small>Y</small> first recollected vision—a patchwork quilt in my aunt's bedroom—is suddenly transformed into a night piece by the river. With my brother Michael, I am being led in a crowd to board a ship and pass strange shapes downstairs to a saloon where an astonishing man in evening dress is entrusted with gold watches, such as my father's hunter which would entrancingly fly open when he touched it to my nose. But this man in black and white was permitted to pound them up in his hat and could recover them uninjured from the donors' ears. Much more astonishingly, he ended by setting pigeons and rabbits fluttering and lolloping out of the same wonderful hat. The ship was the *Great Eastern* and these miracles occurred in the winter of 1886 when the great six-masted, four-funnelled paddle ship—the largest ship in the world—lay alongside the North Wall of the Liffey, its insides gutted, its tanks dismantled, its cable-laying days at an end. Lewis of Liverpool had bought Jules Verne's *Floating City* and converted it into a show-boat.

Then my vision explodes into a whole city quarter, a pattern of rectangular streets on the north side of Dublin, slipping down from Mountjoy Square to wide traverses at the foot of the North Circular Road. Here the small boy with his companions had the franchise of quiet streets and with the extraordinary faculty and facility of children perceived and entered into the life of inanimate things. Every street had its own personality, every halldoor and window its own physiognomy, every lamp-post its known number and its allotted role in our existence. Unconsciously, the child grew familiar with these extensions of himself as he was brought to his kindergarten in a convent school near St Francis Xavier's Church in Gardiner Street. The patchwork quilt had become an urban area enshrining a large schoolroom, dappled with classes standing half-hooped about their teachers, and noisily chanting their spelling lessons. He looked down upon them from a little dais reserved for his contemporaries amongst whom he sat occupied with the mathematics of an abacus or some framework of coloured beads, or more aesthetically as part of an orchestra with a ring of bells or a triangle made musical with a steel rod.

Presently street games, games perennial or games seasonal, began to absorb the long afternoons until mealtime came on, and the gas lamps one after the other were lit up. Each had its proper venue determined not by the exigencies of traffic, for there was little or none in our street, but by convenience of site or by weather conditions. Handball was played against a high gable wall at the street corner with scouts to cry 'Nix' or 'Harvey Duff' if any bobby came in sight, for the D.M.P.[1] discouraged ball games. Marbles were played all the year round—casually as when the weather forced us to play in the shelter of an archway; elaborately as when we scooped out a miniature many-holed

1. Dublin Metropolitan Police.

course for 'Hole and Taw', for those were the days before asphalt
had been poured over the land. Marbles graded by material and
size provided the currency for 'swops' or forfeits; they ranged
from cheap stone to highly decorative blown glass, each with its
proper name.

Tops, for no known reason, were seasonal. They included the
peg top, a wooden cone with a strong spike vigorously thrown
into circulation from a close encircling cord, and to be distinguished from its bulging ornate-coloured tin relative—the hum-
ming top given to all children at Christmas—and the less childish
squat spinning top kept going by a whip of slender thongs from
the local cobbler. Kept in violent motion, your object was to
collide with and upset the balance of your opponent; the victor
exacting the usual penalty of trying to split the victim's top by a
fixed number of blows from the steel spike of his own.

But these top games were soon looked down on by growing
lads and relegated to the inferior category of skipping games,
round games, 'tig', hop-scotch and hoops—all perennial and
rather feminine—or rather, not indeed all perennial, for with the
disappearing coopers' trade these tall, light, spring hoops,
elegantly controlled by a hooked steel handle, have now vanished
from our streets.

Our favourite Dublin street games were ball games: rounders
or such concerted running games as prisoners' base which we
called by its triumphant shout 'RELIEVE-Eee-O!' Two north-
side games still intrigue me by reason of their names. I do not
think they are played in the country and they may be not merely
of urban but of foreign origin. One was 'Ball in the Decker'.
But where did this Dublin slang for cap originate? Is it Dutch,
English or Hanoverian? Another game we called 'Charlie across
the Water'. Has this title, this game, a Jacobite origin from the
days when Bonnie Prince Charlie's ships were running the
blockade—who knows? Other games and counting rhymes
suggest races more alien still, immemorial rites and lost languages.

Chestnuts came in autumn when the trees in the squares and the Park were pelted to bring down chestnuts for seasoning in our chimneys. Dried and matured to the right degree of toughness they might become 'conkers', the conquerers of many hard contested duels. Kites came in summer, home-made, with enormous tails of paper twisted into cartridges, or the more ambitious box-kites which soared over the housetops until telephone wires and the E.S.B. ended such urban amenities. Other more sporadic amusements were the mere fashions of a season, like 'diabolo', or came into the streets from circuses or visiting sensationalists. At their challenge our home-made stilts grew higher and higher. We had a season deriving from Spencer Percival, balloonist and parachutist, when every boy's handkerchief was held and tied with a stone into a parachute, or more daringly a sheet or family tablecloth was purloined and converted into a parachute with which we projected ourselves from the tops of lamp-posts or more adventurously from rainpipes and upper window-sills. Most exciting of all were the sports which originated from the visits of Mexican Joe and his Red Indians and cowboys to Jones's Road (now Croke) Park. At every corner fierce Sioux and gallant cowboys with bows and arrows, pistols, squibs and 'scutterbullies' raided and rescued the stage-coach.

All our games ended by tea-time. The approach of that hour usually found us drifting down Jones's Road to the old whiskey distillery of the D.W.D. Company for the day's finale. There we found a line of carts beginning to pass, one by one, under a great chute, where fascinated we watched each in turn brimmed over by the shining flood of warm grain. The air was heavy with that familiar smell which pervaded whole sections of the city when the wind was from the west and we were glad to run from it a hundred yards further to the canal and railway bridge to feast on a sight more wonderful still. Slow moving on the upgrade and enormously long, puffing smoke, rattling and groaning, the six o'clock goods train passed under our admiring eyes, marvellously equipped with two engines, one in front and the other at the rear. Sated with the spectacle and the Angelus ringing, we scattered to our homes.

The friendly milkman, generous with jaunts, had meanwhile made us acquainted with the grasslands beyond the canal bridges, from Drumcondra and Glasnevin to Santry and in mid-summer we explored the banks of the Tolka and returned with our jam-jars stocked with 'pinkeens' and sticklebacks. These were carefully examined for future 'champions' reared in the dark to become the ferocious victors in other duels and winning much spoil in marbles or other coveted wealth for their fortunate masters. So the seasons mellowed into autumn when we would repair to Donnelly's orchard in Clonliffe Road to fill our caps with apples for a penny, harbingers of Hallow's Eve and indoor entertainment. But before winter set in and the first longed-for snow fell it was still fascinating to wander through the darkening streets from sweetshop to sweetshop, each with its own speciality, each the terminus of our dwindling finances. Chocolates were not in great supply, but bars of cream chocolate were in demand when funds stood high, and when they were low there were always jelly sticks at a farthing each, and liquorice twist like boot-laces that were easily divisible for sharing out or could be stored in your pockets for school use. Bullseyes, butterscotch, Peggy's leg, barley sugar twisted like the pillars of Bernini's baldachino held the middle ground; best of all toffee, the stickier the better. The smallest shop had its speciality. Except for 'lucky bags' there was no shiny packaging. You saw what you bought, and what processing there was you saw as it went on in the back parlour of the shop. From there came slabs of toffee, ruby as stained glass, and brittle at first, but ultimately as engaging to the molar and as enduring as glue. There was an inferior granular type, less tenacious, made by a little old lady in Emmet Street who later distressingly died in its composition, falling over the frying pan into her fire in the back parlour of the shop.

The shopkeepers, even those into whose premises we trailed with our mothers, were our personal friends, and at Christmas they recompensed us for our custom in the gift hampers that came from them—for our seniors a bottle of whiskey, a bottle or port, a bottle of sherry and a madeira cake, for us a barm brack, biscuits, raisins and tangerines.

To wander down Summerhill was something of an adventure for a ten-year-old. The residential area from Mountjoy Square to the North Circular Road, although it was rapidly decaying, in my first decade was open, airy and well-kept. Mountjoy Square, a generation in age later than Rutland Square, was built as a haven from the noisy traffic from north County Dublin which once flowed into the city through Dorset Street and Bolton Street, but had begun to pass down Rutland Square. Its residents when I first knew it were mainly lawyers, with a judge or two, and a couple of wine merchants whose houses, I was told, had cellars extending beneath the roadway towards the centre of the Square. There were still carriage folk amongst them, but for the most part they made their dignified way into town on foot, and there was one old lady of a still earlier generation who was preceded by a footman with a tall cane, when she took the air. But that upper road was little used by me, who, even after kindergarten, had no business in that direction beyond Gardiner Street Church. And I had little business beyond Summerhill, which made the lower and shorter approach to the city, except during Holy Week to the Pro-Cathedral in Marlborough Street, and at all times to a schoolmate whose father owned a coach-building establishment in Findlater's Place next door to Rush, the cab and car proprietor mentioned in Joyce's *The Sisters*. Neville's, like Hutton's, Lafayette's, Briscoe's and Farrell's, made this area one of the very few surviving centres of what was once a great Dublin industry. The superb relics of our eighteenth-century coach-building were later show-pieces of the National Museum, challenging the work of any metropolis.

14

Now neglected and hidden, they moulder in the Royal Hospital.

In 1890 my friend's family lived, as was the fashion of those days, in the establishment they owned, and its yard, with the lofts and galleries around it, its horses, carriages and harness made a fascinating playground for youth. To get to it, my brother and I passed the raised terraces of modest houses and the walled embankments where the top of Summerhill had at some date been shaven off and new levels contrived. At one time it had been a picturesque countrified approach from the city to the sea. Then under the impetus of Beresford's building at the Custom House, high five-storey houses were built here in the late eighteenth century. Less splendid, indeed, than those in Mountjoy Square, they commanded fine views across the bay towards the Dublin mountains. Up to the middle of the nineteenth century there were aristocratic names amongst the attorneys who lived there, but when we knew these houses they were decaying into tenements. Yet, as if remembering its old name of Farmer's Hill, and the existence there of the old Farming Society, the district, like Thomas Street on the south side, always maintained a half-city, half country-town activity, and this may be one reason why coachbuilders, livery establishments and farriers congregated there. In my schooldays a few solicitors lived in these houses, and in their midst, like a cameo in a tarnished ring, an ancient professor of classics. Opposite in their shadow, but undismayed, a new agglomeration of little shops confronted them, sweetshops, tallow chandlers, dairies, public houses, bakeries, greengrocers and provision shops—above all provision shops. And as we made our way home in the autumn evenings the fan-tailed gas jets hissed and flared in every window over their stocks of pigs' cheeks, 'whisperers' and crubeens, sheep's heads and trotters, tripe and vegetables—untidy cornucopias that poured their store across doorways hung with great boards of dried ling, hollow carcasses of oxen and hanks of onions, on to the crowded pathway to a vociferous fringe of basket-women in the gutter selling their apples and herrings.

This noisy disarray was a contrast to our quiet street, only ten minutes' trot away. There was little traffic there, and every wheeled thing that came had its hour and was our friend. First to arrive was the milkman. The rattling of his churn-shaped, brass-bound milk cans and the clatter of his pot measure on the front doorsteps signalled a new day begun. In summer he drove in from his fields at Santry, but in winter not so far away, for cattle could then still be kept in the back lanes of the city, and he had a stable in Rutland Lane. He drove a sort of dogcart, back to back to his pair of gleaming milk cans, and he filled his long spouted pail from the taps which projected through the back board. Into our jugs, twice a day, went the measure of milk and after the measure there invariably went with it the milkman's 'tilly' to compensate for any possible foaming deficiency. Then came the breadman in time for breakfast—bakers then worked night shifts—in the high van which is still occasionally to be seen in our streets. Descending from his lofty perch, he swung open the wings of his van, where shelves of loaves, steaming from the oven, were flanked by other racks, filled with a rivalry of crumpets and barm bracks. Later came coalmen with their bells, and the regular itinerants: the sturdy fishwomen carrying baskets on their heads, on a rolled pad, with cod, hake and mackerel, and the herring women crying 'fresh Dublin Bay herrings'. Other basket women came crying their wares in due season, 'shamrock, sweet shamrock', freshwater cress, strawberries on cabbage leaves, and other small fruit or mushrooms. On his regular day the glazier passed by with panes of glass fitted into the framework he carried on his back, and the knifegrinder with his wheel, sure of his custom. These were the arabesques of domestic economy, useful to housekeeping. The itinerant musicians were of greater interest to the small boy. Amongst them the German bands ranked highest. I do not know what impulse of *Volkerwanderung* or *Drang*

Nach Westen drove them first to our shores, but they were very familiar to our street in the 'nineties; ten or twelve of them at a time, serious and bespectacled in blue jackets and stiff peaked caps, their music cards stuck in their instruments, blowing lustily in a ring. I heard them for the last time in 1913 from Ross's Hotel in Kingstown as it was then called. Our Cui Bono dining club was sitting in a window recess when, seeing them pass, Tom Kettle called to them and, unconscious of doom, they played to us one familiar student song after another.

As welcome was the hurdy-gurdy man, his barrel organ twanging and stammering through 'Santa Lucia' with its gapped teeth while his two lovebirds selected the card which held your fortune. He was far more popular when he was fully equipped with his monkey gaily dressed in a zouave jacket, red trousers, and a pillbox or peaked cap on his head. With melancholy indifferent eyes the monkey would stretch out for his dues, or somersault for them to the ground. Then, there was also the talented one-man band who accompanied his wind instruments with drum and cymbals on his back, the one played by sticks fastened to his elbows, the clashing cymbals by strings from his ankles. The tin whistlers were of small account, hardly distinguishable from the beggars who had their fixed day for calling for their understood ration. Most popular of all our street entertainers was Jack the Tumbler, a hairy black-bearded little roly-poly of a man, in a hat without a brim who, followed by a train of admirers, rolled along the pavement for pennies. He rolled along the roadway too, in all weathers, following outside cars, but the poor fellow, who was said to have been once an umbrella maker, had little for his pains, dying in the Union. Another such character, whom I dimly remember seeing far out at Powerscourt, was Billy the Bowl, a legless cripple who propelled himself and his little vehicle with short pegs. He had adopted his name and means of transport from a disreputable eighteenth-century predecessor, a criminal type who ended his days in jail, or on the gallows. Our Billy was honest and played the tin whistle for excursionists to the Dargle or Powerscourt waterfall. At the lowest level in our scale were the rag and bone merchants, who discouraged by our parents, swopped 'wind-mills' or bullseyes with us for bottles and jam jars.

Then the evening closed in and at nightfall in bed we could still see. One heard the last of the street cries as the cockle man came up from Clontarf or across the river from the Shelly Banks. More lonely than the curlew's cry in a high-pitched monotone his single call went up, 'Cock. . . .les', as if wailing the dirge of his trade in sea food, once celebrated in Dublin song, but now fallen into disfavour by reason of a medical report on the condition of the river's mouth.

These were our visitors, but of more serious communal interest were the doctors who came in their broughams to our neighbours or ourselves. Most sensational amongst them, for ample reason, was Dr Meldon who chose to drive a 'fly' or hansom. Dr Meldon was famously obese, as famous for his weight as the end man in the tug-of-war team of the Dublin Metropolitan Police, who held the world's championships in or about 1893. We all knew Dublin's joke about Dr Meldon getting out from a fly—a greater miracle than Jonah's emergence from the belly of the whale. The commonalty, however, used cabs. Their appearance meant the arrival or departure of country visitors, a dance or theatre party, but best of all when, sent to fetch one from the nearest hazard, we returned in it to assist in loading it up with the enormous trunks that made provision for our annual holiday. Outside cars were for solo flights and for cutting a dash to the races, but the coming of the bicycle ended their use for Sunday excursions to the Dargle or the Strawberry Beds.

A more curious Sunday habit combined excursions with funerals. In Dublin funerals used to be a sort of popular pageantry and the long strings of outside cars passing up O'Connell Street to Glasnevin Cemetery on Sundays were a very familiar sight.

Not all the passengers, seated three aside on the car, were mourners. It is only a few years ago that a friend of mine, travelling in Hungary, was asked by a native to explain something that had left him mystified ever since he happened to be a tourist in Dublin. On a Sunday, at midday, he chanced to be standing on the sidewalk near a great column in the principal street, watching a funeral pass. One of the cars with only two passengers drew up and he was invited, without any more ado, to join them. He mounted beside them, fearing that any failure to do so might imply some disrespect. He described a cheerful progress to what was obviously the gate of a cemetery, which they did not enter, but after a respectful pause they continued their drive for two or three miles to a village where they went into a tavern and spent a pleasant hour or two before returning to the city. The afternoon's entertainment cost him nothing, but left him wondering what this singular funeral meant. He admired the hospitality extended to a foreigner. He was not aware that many a Sunday funeral was a free-for-all, or rather that the jarvey could fill his car at eight pence a seat, and that Flood's at Finglas was the recognized terminus.

Such divagations were not for us, but as time went on our treks extended to the heart of the city, rarely to Grafton Street, and never beyond the ducks in Stephen's Green. Our journeys were usually purposeful and conducted by our elders. We were brought to the bootmaker to be measured yearly for the pair of boots which made life a torment for a week, or more agreeably to the grander drapers where the aerial railways, with a click, hoisted your money in a two-piece cricket ball to the main line, sent it miraculously on its way to the cashier in the distant gallery, whence more marvellously still it picked its way back through the wire netway of diverging tracks, came to its appropriate siding, paused like a helicopter, dropped your change into the shop assistant's hands. These delights, however, were in bad weather hardly bought with the discomfort of the long trail through muddy streets. Difficult now to realize the virtue of asphalt. In the 'nineties one was ever and always scraping one's boots and stockings and cleaning them when dry from the caked mud of the town. The grown-ups were in worse case, whose skirts, petticoats and trouser ends were in perpetual need of attention. On tram routes the Dublin United Tramway Company paved with half sets the space between their rails. Everywhere else the roadway was at the mercy of iron-shod traffic, and in bad weather was churned into mud. Vain as the strivings of Sisyphus were the efforts of the bootblacks with their brushes at work at their stools under the portico of the Bank of Ireland and of the G.P.O.; as vain the efforts of the street cleaners on the pavements of O'Connell Bridge and College Green, pushing ripples of mud before them as they advanced with their wide, rubber rakes, or of their horse-drawn colleagues who swept the roadway, manoeuvring the slant of their bristling cylinders to lessen the menace of the grey flood. No, November to March, out of doors, was a grim tunnel with few skylights. Release from it was only by favour of a hard winter such as we had in 1894 when snowballing went on to Easter, and we could slide up the Canal past the passenger fly-boats rotting at Mountjoy, and away beyond the lock at the Pin Mills by open stretches as far as Ashtown and Blanchardstown. Christmas, even out of doors, was a different story, starred by our ritual visits to the cribs in the city churches, and most signally to the oriental, panoramic groupings of the crib at Inchicore. We found other reward in the rivalry of the shops who competed in the animation of clockwork figures playing out their elaborate set pieces. Finally, on Christmas Eve in convoy of the wisest of parents, we penetrated to Thomas Street to see the even then disappearing open-air market to which County Wicklow came in with all its feathered population lining the streets with holly-festooned stands, trestles and uptilted carts until, tired, we returned as a last exhilaration by way of Patrick Street where, before one side was demolished and the Cathedral

Close opened up, the old-clothes dealers in the narrow street, and the coffin makers of Cork Street swarmed out to join the hurdy-gurdy men making festival till midnight with their barrel-organs.

Let the cosmic physicists say what they will, the seasons in these early 'nineties were sharply distinguished. Winter was winter with snow and chilblains. Summers were hot, and their spectacular thunderstorms could be as confidently reckoned on in late June as our school examinations. Air conditioned as we were, we could accommodate ourselves. Anyway, one of our greatest delights was not seasonal. Hengler's Circus was no mere *Cirque d'Hiver*. True, it may have first come to my town as a travelling show, but when I knew it in the Rotunda Gardens it was built to last and the show went on. The Henglers were a family of seasoned and versatile performers, ringmasters, tight-rope walkers and dainty equestriennes. The Hengler who built and owned the circus was, I have been told, ringmaster in Batty's, an older circus in Abbey Street. But more than their skill in performance we relished the special features whose diversity kept the regular programme fresh. There was Whimsical Walker with his donkey; there was Handy Andy who did his valiant best, in spite of the ringmaster, to help his colleagues, and by assistance dislocated them, but there were also the new features. There was Dick Turpin's Ride to York (oh, rare Turpin, oh) on Black Bess who, having triumphantly surmounted every conceivable obstacle, died in the end so pathetically in the arms of her grief-stricken master; there was the gallant and more contemporary Defence of Rorke's Drift against the Zulus, and again, the ever memorable Water Novelty when the whole ring was filled by gushing water hoses and then occupied by punts and gondolas, in perpetual trouble while Whimsical Walker sat fishing from the ringside, imperturbable through all this commotion and immobile save for his face which lit up and clouded over as hope rose and faded.

The nights then were not obliterated by the long twilights of summer-time, but instead of this Joshua-like staying of the sun in the sky, fireworks and fairy lamp-lit band promenades prolonged our Saturday evenings, whether by the sea or at charity bazaars like *Araby* or after athletic carnivals. We were beginning to interest ourselves in athletics. We kept our eye on the world's champions and demonstrated on each other the punches of John L. Sullivan. All the world champions were, of course, Irish—except for accident—and we went to see them at Ballsbridge and Clonturk Park. We had long been encountering the Clonliffe Harriers padding sturdily through the winter dusk from the Phoenix Park down the North Circular Road or further afield, cross-country in north County Dublin. Now we could see their picked men, Tommy Conneffe and Joe Lahiff, on the cinder track, in the company of our greatest favourites, the cyclists. Dubliners were then as mad on cycling as any of the present day votaries of the *Tour de France*. We knew we were first in the field. Living in the days of Dunlop and Du Cros we watched the progress of cycling from the cradle to the grave. We saw the high bicycle and the penny-farthing competing with the low bicycle at Ballsbridge, and the solid tyre outpassed by the non-detachable pneumatic. We watched the great succession of R. J. Mecredy, L. J. O'Neill and Harry Reynolds and Bob Stevens, catching half lemons in their stretched pocket handkerchiefs, as they pedalled their fifty miles round the Park, or lapping up world records on the Ballsbridge track, while Ryan was asserting equal supremacy at the hammer-and weight-throwing, and the D.M.P. tug-of-war team stretching indomitable muscles along the rope, the 'Baby of the Force' its monumental end-man.

Our sports were on sea as well as on land. A chain of regattas linked the coast from Skerries to Arklow and the paddle boats, the *Erin's Queen* or *Erin's King*, helped our transport from the Custom House Quay. The Clontarf and Ringsend regattas were at first far enough and good enough for us, perhaps because our interest was not mainly nautical. It centred on the final events; on the greasy pole erected as a mast or extended from the bowsprit, which was climbed or gingerly traversed by competitors rigged out as clowns who sought to clutch the sucking pig or ham suspended at the top; or in the free-for-all duck hunt when the birds were released amongst the boats with a wild flutter of wings and the winners swam back triumphantly, disdaining the flurry, with the duck's bill in their teeth.

Terrestrial or maritime, these sports were, as I have said, enlivened with brass bands and fireworks, and inevitably both had a political colouring. On the south side, at Kingstown or Dalkey the music, by kind permission of the colonel and officers, was regimental, though a pot-pourri by Dan Godfrey with 'St Patrick's Day' might be included in the programme of military marches and Gilbert and Sullivan. Closer in to the heart of the city the St James's Brass and Reed Band played unmistakable national airs. Ballsbridge was neutral with the band of the Dublin Metropolitan Police. Similarly with the fireworks. Nothing in the way of aerial beauty and crepitating brilliance could compare with those fiery sheaves of light and gorgeous set pieces. The Fête of St Louis at Versailles or such-like displays on the Seine seen in later years, had little or nothing on Clonturk Park or Ballsbridge. But, with us, as no doubt elsewhere, the occasion was carefully gauged. Erin go Bragh with harp and shamrocks as a set piece on the south side would fade into the extensive portrait of Queen Victoria before it at length guttered into final darkness. On the north side we preferred the Harp and Parnell flanked by William O'Brien and John Dillon. But with the Parnell split this iconography also faded.

I find it impossible to pin down the moment when we became conscious of such political differences. Wars abroad were a separate matter. They were exciting events which took place at a distance in time as well as space, and they could provide material for special attractions at Hengler's Circus. The Defence of Rorke's Drift, for example, kept us *au courant* twenty years after, with the Zulu War. We learned from it how an Irish V.C. with a handful of dying comrades behind sand bags long kept at bay Cetewayo and his impes hurling their assegais as they charged in the shelter of their long striped shields of leopard skin. Even at Hengler's our feelings were torn—divided between Irish valour which was taken as a matter of course, and the flag and dubious cause with which it was unfortunately associated. More remote in time, the images of another war filled our wet Sunday afternoons when, flat out on the drawing-room floor, my brother and I studied the illustrated pages of Cassell's *History of the Franco-German War*. From amongst its pictures of protagonists we had picked our special favourites, but we were not greatly tied by political considerations. There was more than a semblance of neutrality—for however much we would have liked to be on the winning team, the Marshal with an Irish name, MacMahon, was with the losers. We could admire the ascetic figure of Moltke and (because they were Catholics) share the triumph of the bearded Bavarians as they marched home, their helmets oak and laurel crowned. We pitied the Marshal, encumbered with a sickly Emperor, himself wounded; hoped for the best with Gambetta when he took his place in the balloon that rose from the beleagured capital; and deplored the wild fury of the *petroleuses*. We made little of the small print which gave the lengthy despatches of Russell Forbes and the other war correspondents, but enough of Cassell's two volumes to give lads not yet in their teens an intelligent interest in modern Europe.

This was war and the world from a distance. At home we heard hardly intelligible talk of land troubles and the goings and comings of, to us, unknown personalities. My first recollection of a political demonstration is still unclear. It was at night, a torchlight procession with bands and cheering crowds seen in North Frederick Street, convoying William O'Brien or John Dillon or Michael Davitt to or from the Broadstone Station. What I do

remember is my mother's tears when, a year or two later, we
came back from school with the news of Parnell's death, and then
his funeral passing us where his statue now stands in O'Connell
Street. I was then eight years old, but shared the misery in the
faces about me and the desperate, angry sorrow that filled the
streets. At home, as in so many Irish families, my father and
mother took different sides in the Parnell split, but their unbroken
affection and good sense brought them to a quick compromise by
which politics of the 'split' were no longer mentioned in the
house, but each took in the newspaper of what each regarded as
the appropriate colour. That, too, was ultimately good for growing boys, but Dublin was predominantly Parnellite, and knowing
nothing of the issues I fell in with the other boys who sang as they
passed his door on Mountjoy Square:

> We'll hang Tim Healy on a sour apple tree
> As we go marching along.

If we were yet ill equipped to judge national politics we could
still take our part in municipal affairs. Anything that brought the
fire brigade into the street brought us out with them—and anything in the way of bands, banners and processions. It was so we
assisted at the unveiling of Father Mathew's statue in O'Connell
Street just as it was our annual duty to assist at the inaugural
procession of the Lord Mayor. Our favourite viewpoint was on
the lower slope of Rutland Square. Here we saw the Lord Mayor
pass in cocked hat and fur gown, seated in the carved gilt city
coach drawn by three pairs of horses, with outriders. He was
preceded by the City Marshal on horseback, and by another
coach with the city mace and the city sword projecting from the
windows. His own equipage shone magnificiently, for it was
up to each Lord Mayor on assuming office to have the coach
refurbished by Hutton the coachbuilder on Summerhill, as well
as to provide a new brougham and liveries for his men. But it

was when the city magnates passed that the procession reached, for us, its climax. Our favourite section—the fire brigade—halted a little lower down, at the Rotunda—where, in the days of the horse trams, their little postillion used to stand his auxiliary tram horse, ready to yoke it swiftly to the pair straining to mount the slope. Now there was a pause to give space for the dashing manoeuvre when Dublin's Fire Brigade charged the hill. It was led by Captain Purcell in his dogcart behind a spanking pair of perfectly groomed horses, his little fox terrier barking furiously. Then followed, with bells clanging, the brigade and their fire engines drawn by pairs of galloping horses; the men standing erect, brass-helmeted, in red blouses and shining boots, and all their equipment, culminating in the fire ladders gleaming, while all the time the horses' hooves thundered and struck fire from the paving sets.

This resounding and brilliant spectacle reduced to insignificance the Lord Mayor's official convoy of furred and moth-eaten Aldermen and Councillors in their open landaus whose names, growing familiar to us, we recited often with unflattering epithets. But even Captain Purcell's merry men did not put the picturesque Irish National Foresters out of countenance. Remembering, perhaps, Little John's association with Oxmantown, this worthy benevolent society used to march in an earlier generation behind a banner of Robin Hood and Little John embellished with the trophies of woodland chase. As we saw them pass, Robert Emmet held the field. The scarved members were preceded and flanked by a splendid cavalcade in the Robert Emmet costume which coloured lithographs had made no less familiar than St Patrick's. They wore dark green, wide brimmed felt hats with white plumes, green cutaway coats with epaulettes and gilt buttons, white knee-breeches, and riding boots. At their head, mounted on a Shetland pony, rode a little girl with golden ringlets, dressed in the same attire. Year after year the Dublin crowd waited for her apparition, changed but unchanged. They cheered her, loudly

26

recognizing any singularity in her followers; loved, laughed at and admired their gallant incongruity.

If we did not take the Aldermen and Foresters too seriously, we did take careful stock of the great trade banners which headed each section of the trade unions. The trades of Dublin made the bulk of the procession, and from our standpoint on Rutland Square we had a complete vista of their banners. Mounted on floats, they advanced slowly like frigates in full sail from O'Connell Street. The banners were enormous, rising twenty feet into the air, and we read them attentively as they laboured by. Men in low-crowned hats, with scarves or sashes, stood holding the guyropes, others marched alongside keeping guard. The canvasses were painted front and back. Corded, tasselled and fringed in green and gold, they swung in their frames, some, like that of the wood workers, elaborately carved with fluted pillars and classical capitals and entablatures, others with pike heads as posts and with arched tops surmounted by harp, round tower or wolfdog.

The banners were almost all of canvas, but some were of silk or poplin. The front usually bore the patron saint of the trade, or Erin with her romantic accessories, or some Irish historical figure set in a familiar landscape. On the reverse the arms of the trade would be heraldically displayed with scrolls and mottoes supported by allegorical figures of Justice, Concord, Hope, Commerce and so forth, or at least with their emblems and often with an entertaining variety of relevant fauna. Stallions romped with the tanners and saddlers; eagles, pheasants and rabbits accompanied the poulterers. I can recall among the patron saints the painters' banner with St Luke painting the Blessed Virgin, the carpenters' St Joseph with his chisel and mallet, the butchers with the Agnus Dei bearing a cross, and the shoemakers with St Crispin. Forty years after these early processions my friends in the Plasterers' Guild unrolled for me in their hall in Essex Street their high banner of St Bartholomew painted by Mannix of

Bachelor's Walk. Favourite history pieces were St Patrick on his mountain, with shamrock and snakes and Brian Boroimhe on a charger with his battle-axe. Clontarf, Glendalough, Killarney, were the usual landscape settings. Other banners that remain in my memory had biblical or mythological figures. The Operative and Amalgamated Tailors had greatly admired rival banners, the one showing the temptation of Adam and Eve, the other the expulsion from the Garden of Eden. Dan O'Connell saw, but I arrived too late to see, an earlier *tableau vivant* of the tailors, presenting Adam and Eve in flesh tights with a big apple tree standing in a hogshead, just as the bakers showed seven barrels of flour and a breadman on each. The bricklayers combined the Pyramids and the Pantheon with the old Parliament House in College Green and Ross Castle, Killarney. The smiths showed Vulcan at his forge; others had more modern operatives at work.

O'Connell gave a new and special character to these processions. He gave precedence to his bodyguard of coalporters over the portly merchants of the Holy Trinity. Their banner was guarded by stalwarts in black armour whose vizors gave them trouble when later they sought much-needed refreshment. The erection of the loopline railway bridges made it impossible for them to carry their tall, proud banner any longer, but the coalporters maintained their precedence to my own day. Even still, as members of the Transport and General Workers' Union, their band leads our civic demonstrations. It was to O'Connell's aggregate Repeal meetings that we owed both a new departure in trade banners, and the popularity of the bands that enlivened our scene. Sir Charles Gavan Duffy noted that these pipe and drum bands were quite unknown to the countryside of his youth. They were fostered, if not set up, by Father Mathew as part of his temperance crusade. Multiplied and enlisted by O'Connell to play their spirited part at his Repeal meetings, these bands— whether brass or pipe and drum—remained a feature of all later demonstrations.

Proud of their ancestry, the trades yet held on to the 'antique and learned imagery' of their fathers. The designers of these banners married their allegories and insignia with our national heroes, and small boys learned from their colour more than they gathered from emasculated national school textbooks. The banners of the inaugural processions became a moving mosaic of our history, and since they were constantly added to, or superseded as generations changed, historians could judge what figures made the strongest or most immediate appeal to popular affection. In the early 'nineties—presided over by Erin, the green flag and gold harp, the sunburst and round tower, Irish cross and wolfdog —Brian Boroimhe, O'Connell, Emmet and Lord Edward easily held the first place. Moore's melodies filled the air with their music and the banners with their embellishments. Grattan and the old Parliament were also present, Wolfe Tone hardly appeared, and so far as I remember, the '48 men not at all. Davis, Mitchel and Duffy were literary figures only. With 'God save Ireland' the Land League men, Parnell, O'Brien, Dillon and Davitt then came memorably on the scene, but not on the same spectacular scale as on the earlier banners. The old craft was apparently dying out and their smaller portraits—save for an occasional Parnell, erect with folded arms—were set with eviction scenes reminiscent of the *Weekly Freeman* and *United Irishman* cartoons. The '98 centenary introduced Wolfe Tone and Father Murphy of Wexford and Cave Hill took its place with the Rock of Cashel. At the same time, two outside elements interfered materially to disturb and eventually to end the old order. The loopline railway bridges in and about the city had already narrowed the field of manoeuvre for the lofty banners, but when our horse-drawn trams were electrified, the new wires, in their turn, proved an impossible obstacle and regretfully we came to the end of these towering parades.

Their decline corresponded with a change in the date and character of the mayoral display. Hitherto it had taken place on St

Patrick's Day. For some reason the date was changed, and when the Gaelic League succeeded in making St Patrick's Day a public holiday, the mayoral inauguration had shrunk to insignificance and the Gaelic League took over control and supplied a pictorial replacement. The trades still marched with the Gaelic League branches, but without their banners. In their places the Gaelic League introduced—for a few years successfully—a picturesque didactic scenario of Irish history. Practised in stage craft, they mounted tableaux on the old floats: Cuchulainn and the Red Branch, Finn and Oisin, Deirdre and the Children of Uisneach, the Four Masters at work on their annals, Geoffrey Keating in his Galtee cave writing his history, Davis, Duffy and Dillon founding *The Nation*. Small boys who had seen Adam and Eve pass by with Vulcan, O'Connell and Robert Emmet were now themselves lending a hand to this new iconography. They found the Dublin workmen at first rather shyly but later with jealous alacrity donning new disguises to relive a past in which history and mythology, fact and fiction, were still curiously blended. It ended with the labour strikes and lockouts of 1913, the Easter Rising, pipers' bands, kilts and drum majorettes.

This was how history came down into the streets in my school-days. It will be gathered that in our school we took no stock of the British garrison or of Lord Lieutenants. We did not lift our caps to them in the streets or on any occasion stoop to the trooping of their colours in the Upper Castle Yard. Yet it should be confessed that we were not bigoted doctrinaires, and by common indulgence we permitted ourselves one deviation. 'The twenty-fourth of May, the Queen's Birthday' was a bank holiday, and our school, not unwillingly, accepted the situation. On that day we hurried out to the Phoenix Park to see the military review in the Fifteen Acres. That magnet was as irresistible as the fire brigade. Viceregal varletry was there in parasols, silk hats and victorias. Unregarding, we passed through them to the front lines from which we watched the military evolutions. We heard the click of bayonets along the extended files. We waited for the dropping musketry fire as it ran down the 'thin red lines' and watched them forming squares against the cavalry, kneeling and standing, sputtering fire as at Waterloo. We quivered with terrible delight at the thunder of artillery, right of them and left of them, until at length the squares dissolved and the lines opened up, and we manfully, with not unreasonable confidence, faced the culminating charge of the lancers as they bore down, hell for leather, upon our very noses. It was as good as Major de Robeck blaspheming his County Kildare team to victory on the polo ground across the road, and almost as good as Captain Purcell on his dogcart clattering over the 'sets' at the head of his fire brigade, his fox terrier furiously barking.

2   The Birth of Taste

A T school we found O'Connell keeping company with Lord
Edward as on the trade banners. Ours was the O'Connell
School, North Richmond Street, a five minutes' trot from the
house where the schoolboy was born and lived out his first twelve
years. O'Connell himself had laid its foundation stone in 1828,
the year before Emancipation. His bust is on the façade and a
little school museum, cased around the vestibule, held relics of
history and geology; our favourite specimen was the wavy,
leaf-shaped dagger with which, it was said, Lord Edward
Fitzgerald resisted arrest by Major Sirr in 1798. Established by the
Christian Brothers, this day school gave both primary and secondary education, and was, I should think, the most frequented
school in Ireland. As in all the schools of the Irish Christian
Brothers, the primary teaching stood quite apart from the state
system of national schools which, even when they had thrown
off Dr Whatley's proselytising efforts, retained to the end an

artificially negative attitude to Irish convictions. The schools of the Christian Brothers were explicitly Catholic and Irish, using their own excellent textbooks and preserving and developing the normal atmosphere of life outside their walls. Their secondary education was harmonized with the later established Intermediate educational system. Year after year the teaching in the O'Connell School, assisted no doubt in great part by dint of numbers, kept it foremost in the public competitive examinations of the Inter-mediate Board. The Brothers became in fact past masters in the techniques of competitive examinations. They never lost, or weakened, in their original purpose, but accommodation with the universally accepted curriculum did tend to a certain routine in teaching that was amply compensated in the variety of their pupils. The pupils were day boys only, but they made a fairly complete cross-section of the urban population. Few came from legal or medical families, though indeed one of my older com-rades, later our City Treasurer, sat for a period beside Oliver St John Gogarty in fascinated terror of a brandished scalpel purloined from his father's surgery. My class fellows were drawn from the families of civil servants and shopkeepers, Corporation officials, market salesmen and County Dublin farmers—notable amongst them Tom Kettle who arrived each morning in a gig, driven in from his father's farm in north County Dublin. When he left for Clongowes the continuity of history was maintained by Ned Kent (Eamonn Ceannt) later executed in the Easter Rising of 1916, and then by Michael Davitt's son, Cahir, who was to be President of the High Court under the Republic. My own class was a heterogeneous lot who filled up school and out-of-school hours with diverse interests. Ned Kent was a natural leader, an initiator and austere personality, whom I recollect in class as a tall, pale youth, rather awkward and deceptively shy, but our admitted arbiter on points of schoolboy honour. My friend, Stephen McKenna, the translator of Plotinus, served with him as an Irish Volunteer, and likened him to a remote and

33

C

tranquil harvest moon, but also to a good-humoured uncle telling his nephews to use their little fists for their rights like little men. I also have relics of such an avuncular relationship when in my late college days this single-minded ascetic reproached me with my inadequate knowledge of Irish and summoned me to join him in starting a North City suburban Gaelic League class.

By that time he had learned the pipes. Once, being of a party of Irish pilgrims visiting Rome, he put on the kilt—that pretended Irish traditional dress—and to the amazement of the Pope and half-scandalized members of his Curia, marched up and down the Cortile di San Damaso playing 'The Coolin' and war marches. There is no better description of him than this passage by Stephen McKenna which I cannot but transcribe from Professor E. R. Dodd's *Memoir* of McKenna, so accurate is it and characteristic of both men:

'I cannot quite think of the pipes with the calm acceptance one offers the violin or even the flute, when a long grave man—well dressed, of religious mien, a native philosopher and mystic, showing in his luminous face and solemn presence the race of which he is sealed—stands massively on the platform of a garishly lighted hall before a vast audience that has just been yelling with exaltation and defiance over political speeches; when with thoughtful deliberation he takes the pipes from a gill, arranges the curious tubes and bags, elaborately tunes, solemnly begins to play—why, may the outraged spirit of the ancient spirit absolve me—such a sight would normally make me smile. None the less, one of my cherished memories is of Eamonn Ceannt piping just so at the Antient Concert Rooms a short time before the Rebellion. There had been eloquent haranguing, fiery response from the Hall, the thrill of an Ireland resurgent to virile plans and passionate hopes. During an interval princely Eamonn rose from the people, gathered his bags and tubes under his wing, tuned, played; and even then, not foreseeing how soon the desperate effort, the tragic end, was coming, even then I felt very sharply, like a knife slashing between the bones, that he stood in some quite rare way as the symbol of the times. That solemnist of all Irish pipers stands and will stand long before my mind like some colossal work of sculpture, some Mestrovitch figure full of the entire meaning of a racial existence.'

Another who sat beside me for two years before my teens, and until his premature death, was a brilliant lad who, more than our teacher, absorbed my attention. I learned from him to fill the margins of our school books with drawings of the Trojan war and Roman history, while he also filled my greedy ears with tales of the Wild West. I was a devotee of *The Boy's Own Paper* but he of *Penny Dreadfuls*. His talk was all of mustangs—fascinating word—bearing heroic cowboys to the rescue from Red Indians of golden-haired maidens. Son of a railway engineer, his father had official residence at the Midland Great Western Station at Broadstone, and there we had the run of the railway works. His house competed with another more distant engineer's house at Inchicore, which had the superior attraction of a Mesmyth hammer which corked bottles for us in the interval of crushing chunks of molten ore in a fountain of sparks. More often Saturday afternoons were spent in Harry Neville's father's coach-building yard in Marlborough Street. Its gallery and lofts held all sorts of gear and the stables were filled with old-fashioned landaus, phaetons, victorias, carriages and brakes, all redolent of horses and harness.

Still more exciting afternoons went at the Bailey Lighthouse, of which the father of another schoolfellow was Keeper. My friend was born on the Blaskets, but now, on the last stronghold of the Norsemen on Howth Head, could proudly display to his envious comrades the brilliant intricacies of his many-faceted 'winking willies'. When such delights failed, autumn brought us to the house of another schoolfellow, a devout student of astronomy. Through a telescope on his roof I first had sight of Saturn, and with him joined in excursions to Dunsink Observatory. Such boyish attractions made no insecure foundation for one's unconscious love of the city and its citizens, and for more regular schooling.

On another plane was our regular frequentation of the Pro-Cathedral during Holy Week. This was in the years before the Palastrina choir was established, but the ceremonies and singing have left their ineffaceable impression. In particular, the Tenebrae service. In the gathering darkness my brother and I made our way down Summerhill and past our friends the coach-builders' yards in Marlborough Street. After a friendly word with Joe Kinahan, a small, dark, baldish clerk of the church, we ran up long flights of stairs to an upper level above the nave, passing in the attic Sweetman or Taylor's wooden model of the original church and so to our favourite seats in the 'half moon', from where we could look down on the crowded congregation, Archbishop Walsh's throne opposite and the students of Clonliffe Seminary in the choir. The stripped altar, its bareness, the gradual extinguishing of the lights in the triangular candlestick, the chanting of the Lamentations and the touching music of the *Improperia* sank into our chastened mood, but we still looked forward to the moment when, the Church plunged in total darkness, the ceremonies commemorating the trembling of the earth by the noisy beating by the students of their service books on the rails of their benches, ended in discordant climax.

They were a distraction from the strict regime of classwork. In the 1890s, school was books all the way to annual examinations. Debating societies were unheard of; athletics were discouraged, but in my day a few school clubs were beginning to make their tentative appearance. I did not shine amongst my fellows either at cricket or as half-back in rugby. I was, on the other hand, perhaps unusually fortunate in my masters. My first encounter was with the Superior, Brother O'Mahony, when I entered school as a child of six. Later I was to meet him in an upper grade, and in between, in the secondary school, he supplemented the usual teacher's half-hour catechetical instruction with more far-ranging lectures. I am still amazed at the ease with which, without any appearance of condescending to tender intelligences, this teacher, cool-smiling, behind his steel-rimmed glasses, could adapt himself to a long course of Church history and hagiography. It amazes me to think that from the age of twelve I was beginning to be acquainted with more than the bare outlines of Church history. In the preparatory grade, I was already growing familiar, not with the names only of St John Chrysostom and Origen, of St Jerome and St Augustine, but with the ebb and flow of early heresies—Donatists, Manichees and Arians. I have learned nothing since to displace what he could unaffectedly impart. Not merely that; his orderly account of saints and heresiarchs was starred with the relevant civil history of the Holy Roman Empire and of France, Spain and Ireland. This amply filled the vacuum in the teaching of European history, for European history, save where England was involved, was completely ignored in the Intermediate curriculum. Mathematics, I have been told, was well taught in my school, but it was a subject little to my taste. I rather liked Euclid and geometry, and tolerated algebra, but sums were to me insoluble and trigonometry an opaque mystery. I still think that Brother O'Mahony's discourse was the main stem and most formative element in our teaching, and a very great part of my generation profited by it. It was adult and not insular.

Other masters have a warm place in my memory; the latest, Brother Maunsel, a vivid personality, understanding himself and his class, and then Brother Swan and Brother O'Connor. In tender years and for a short spell only, until he left us to establish Prior Park in Bath, I had seasonal meetings with Brother Swan. He had been a schoolfellow with Archbishop Walsh in Dr Quinn's famous school in Harcourt Street; was soaked in Old Dublin history and much sought after as a lecturer to Dublin clubs and literary societies. He was a graceful speaker and devoted

37

to elocution; he took charge of the dramatic performances and recitations which went with the usual prize giving. Via Prince Arthur, he was my first introduction, aged ten, to Shakespeare. A longer and more intimate association was with our bearded and beloved Brother O'Connor, son of a government official in India. He was born in India where he also taught until he came to Dublin to our school in his middle years, where, in addition to his regular class work, he took charge of the special school choir. He was a fine musician, and for six or seven years until my voice broke, my musical duties pleasantly interrupted my other class work. Not that I was a distinguished vocalist. I owed my place in the choir to my brother's much superior ability, but I was found quite competent at organ blowing. I pumped the organ every Sunday morning at 7.30 a.m. in the school chapel, singing in a desultory way while attending to the plummet and its scale. In the course of time I rose like a hero in *H.M.S. Pinafore,* and ended my musical career gloriously at the keyboard as the organist for the enlarged choir at Christmas and Easter. Meanwhile, our choir rehearsals were relieved by Brother O'Connor's stories of Hindustani manners and customs; we picked up many Hindustani phrases which went well with the Red Indian stories I had heard in class, and fitted perfectly into Kipling's *Jungle Book* and *Kim* which I was soon to read.

In the primary school also we had the advantage of Vincent O'Brien's supervision, who was the general music master. From the 'modulator', slung over a blackboard, everyone learned tonic-solfa. Whether we could sing well or not we all learned many of Moore's *Melodies* and the result was eminently satisfactory. Our special choir won first place at the newly established Feis Ceoil and we sang at the first Palestrina commemoration in Dublin and sang more Palestrina the next year at the Maynooth College centenary—activities which laid the foundation of the Pro-Cathedral Palestrina choir set up by Archbishop Walsh and Edward Martyn, with Vincent O'Brien as choir master. It is true

that Vincent O'Brien is better known as the first music master of
John McCormack and James Joyce than as mine. But none the less
it was through these masters one came to some knowledge of a
world outside the Intermediate programme.

I reckon my class studied no less than thirteen subjects as we
passed through secondary school. They were chosen and accumulated for their mark-making and prize-winning potential at the
annual competitive exam. I do not regret this wide range which
might seem to involve superficial skimming. It did involve long
school hours and too much home work, but it also made easy
the later choice for specialization. I do not regret a course which
stretched one's study from Latin and two continental languages
through a very full course of mathematics down to shorthand
and book-keeping. But it did exclude the physical sciences except
as alternatives, and made difficult all but the most casual access
to the amenities and green pastures of literature. I find it hard to
discern the birth of taste in this heterogeneous accumulation. By
chance in my case, music had roots in school, but for the general
run it ended peremptorily on admission to the preparatory grade.
Language teaching most often studiously avoided coquetting with
the elegancies of literature. We trod assiduously the arid paths of
syntax. We knew our grammar, our Latin gerunds and ger-
undives, accumulated a vocabulary, could translate French and
German backwards and forwards with whatever correctness we
could command, learned much poetry by heart, including
Shakespeare, and could impose on our essays a rigorous beginning,
middle and end.

Otherwise, as an art, literature hardly existed, either as a
window for the imagination or as a key to the civilization of
other ages or peoples. We plunged, from the age of eleven, into
a strange world of unrelated texts. My earliest recollection, which
I have never checked, remains as a sentence from Cornelius
Nepos: 'Accidit ut Athenienses coloniam ad Chersonesem
mittere voluerunt.' It came from his *Life of Alcibiades* and from

some vague period of Greek history. Otherwise the classics raised problems in geography and syntax—as did those selections from Ovid, Propertius and Catullus which one laboriously construed at the same time. Next year Caesar's *Gallic War* had a fighting interest and the second book of the Aeneid had exciting episodes. But the Latin classics as a whole were all rather a tangle to us, lads of eleven to twelve or thirteen. Lamb's *Tales from the Odyssey* had colour and made sense, but these Romans talking impossible metrics might have been men in the moon.

A similar detachment marked our French texts with a further curiosity in the manner of language teaching. I do not know if it was a method unique to our school, but for five years I learned French without speaking one word of the language. We learned our entire vocabulary and declined our verbs only by spelling aloud *J-e s-u-i-s, t-u e-s,* etc. We pronounced no word or sentence until in our last year a French Christian Brother set matters right, and put us in a more reasonable posture for the university. There was this to be said for the method, that what we learned we learned accurately, and the result was better than Winston Churchill's Harrovian French. Something similar marked our Latin verse composition. At first we shamefacedly ignored this highly marked section of our Intermediate paper. Only in our last year, and under a special teacher, did we take up this queer game of cross-words or linguistic dominoes played out of Smith's Latin Dictionary.

No, not here but further back I can trace the slender trickles which led to the green pastures. In a later chapter I shall have occasion again to mention that quiet man, T. W. Lyster, the Librarian in our National Library. As a lad I met his name as compiler of his *English Poetry for Young Students.* It was a prescribed textbook in our preparatory grade, and I have seen none better fitted to its purpose. Learning it all by rote, and aided by his brief admirable comments, I learned half consciously to love

Goldsmith and Moore, and such cadences as still lie embedded in a remote cell of my brain as Cowper's:

The poplars are felled; farewell to the shade
And the whispering sound of the cool colonnade.

There, too, through Ferguson's *Mesgedra* I learned how my Dublin and its river could be the stuff of history and literature. At another desk in Belvedere—for he had left my school after a very brief period—Joyce was reading the same texts a year earlier. *Mesgedra* was to be one of the day-springs of Anna Livia, flowing through so much of *Finnegans Wake,* and Ferguson's vocabulary may be found recurring in new verbal formations in an early chapter of *Ulysses.* Lamb's *Ulysses* and Fenelon's *Télémaque* were also on our programme in those years. Two years later I met Milton and had 'Lycidas', 'Il Penseroso' and L'Allegro' by heart. Thirty years later, driving with Professor Osborn Bergin, I found myself able to repeat, not all, but long chunks of 'Lycidas'. But Bergin's memory was flawless. When I stumbled or dropped a passage he instantly replaced it. I began to perceive some art in verse writing other than rhyme, and that words could carry overtones like the strings of the violin I was beginning to learn. Our meticulous Latin teacher would quietly insinuate a happier phrase in place of our rough and ready translation. Words had beauty as well as meaning. Horace in my last year might still be difficult, but in spite of syntax and unnecessary periphrasis which only drove one to footnotes essential for examinations, there was an edge to his writing, and shape. He had a place in the world. He made some sense out of classics hitherto only dimly discernible.

None the less, a personal taste is not born at school or greatly developed in the swaddling clothes of a curriculum. Its origins are as obscure as life itself; the seed is born and develops at home. In this I was most fortunate. My friend, Senator Michael Hayes, once said to me that the Dublin artisan of our day was brought up on Moore's *Melodies, The Spirit of the Nation,* and *The Bohemian Girl.* Those I also met in my earliest days and I knew no home of the middle class such as I belonged to, that was without those heavily gilt green and gold volumes lying about the drawing-room. There was also the great Family Bible, and before I could read for myself with any satisfaction I can see myself lying on the floor on wet days, or recuperating from our games, not indeed reading, but turning over its large pages and admiring the steel engravings of Martin R. A. that displayed deluges and lightnings devastating the world, the terraced splendour of Babylon's architecture, and the ruination that fell on all when the strange writing appeared on Belshazzar's palace walls. From these excitements we turned to the pictures in Cassell's *History of the Franco-German War.* They were for many years our trusted resource, until presently I was identifying myself with Ernest, the most indolent but ingenious member of *The Swiss Family Robinson.* My favourite book at twelve or thirteen was one I have never since come across, and I have forgotten its author's name. It was my first independent acquisition from a secondhand bookshop when I hardly knew how to buy a book. It was called *The Swan and Her Crew,* and this fascinating narrative of a boy's holidays in a sailing boat on the Norfolk Broads was plentifully illustrated with woodcuts of unfamiliar birds, crested glebe and the like, and other forms of natural life strange to me outside our Zoo or the Natural History Museum. Some thirty years afterwards W. H. Nevinson told me it was his favourite reading at the same age. I fancy that reprinted, it could still challenge any of our space fiction if only woodcut illustration were as freely used. Then there was Henty from the school lending library, but that store was quickly exhausted. There was more staying power in my father's bookcase even though its books were hard, and except for the pictures, barely intelligible. Still, there was Ball's *Astronomy,* and if it, and texts on electricity and magnetism were plainly above our heads, we became aware of some vague connection between them and our globes, and the pairs of cylinders through which we shivered with delight at the electric shocks my father would administer. These mysteries have always remained mysteries to me, but no book is beyond a child's curiosity, and the bookcase had compensations. My father's liking evidently ran also to history. I still have a few of his calf-bound books—a *History of the Ottoman Empire* and two volumes of Washington Irving's *Spanish Papers*. Their mottled leaves are still very familiar to me. Irving's stories of Don Roderick and the other legendary heroes of Castilian history became great favourites, and I have added little since to what I gleaned of Spain or the Ottoman Turks or the commodores of the early United States Navy from those pages and from his Prescott. I was later to read in his Gibbon and Hallam's *Middle Ages* and a half shelf of translations from Mignet, Guizot and Thiers. More numerous were practical handbooks on carpentry and photography, the hobbies to which he was devoted, and the bound volumes of Cassell's *Popular Educator* and *Technical Educator*. His book buying was, however, slender. His free time was taken up either in the workroom he had fitted up or in a darkroom where he developed his plates, or out of doors in cycling, to which he remained faithfully attached since the days of the penny farthing. I can see him reading only on Sunday evenings when after dinner he would settle down by the fire in his easy chair, a table beside it, upon which 'the materials' had been carefully arranged by his loving wife. The Sunday punch was mixed with ceremony, exactness and joviality. It was the apex of the day, which began with Mass and a long walk in our company and a late afternoon dinner, which left time for our own card playing or music and his reading. His bookcase was therefore, as I have suggested, limited. It was not that my father had no literary taste, but it found its pabulum in history. There was no poetry in that bookcase except a chance Cowper in which I read nothing, a broken-backed Longfellow in which I read extensively, and beside it his translation of Dante, which I found quite unintelligible until I found Irish medieval stories in the small print of its voluminous notes. There was also an extraordinary selection of extracts from Shakespeare called, I think, *The Wisdom and Genius of Shakespeare,* which I found of great use when writing the school essays I hated. Whether by direct quotation or by disguised paraphrase I grew expert in filling up from it my obligatory three-page essay on Punctuality or Honesty is the Best Policy or some such moral theme. There were no novels in that bookcase except *The Count of Monte Cristo.* In it I could find no interest except in the first chapters. I had no use for the love of Mercedes and Dantès, nor any comprehension of the talk of Morcerf and his fashionable friends in Rome and Paris. I found some satisfaction in guessing at the downfall of Dantès's enemies. I liked the pictures; the Count's haughty yet courteous refusal of the grapes proffered by his lost love, the horrible sight of the paralysed procureur, but the picture of the aged Abbé showing Dantès's secret passage to escape from the prison cell in the Château d'If riveted my attention. Rapidly skipping the first pages I read and re-read with never exhausted delight—knowing the happy ending—the narrative of Dantès's imprisonment and escape, and the secret of his great wealth and key to vengeance.

Nor did many novels lie loose about the house. I can only summon up *The Mystery of the Hansom Cab,* Ouida's *Under Two Flags,* with Mark Twain's *Life on the Mississippi,* all yellow backs, and all, save the last, unread by me. There was yet one other— Du Maurier's *Trilby.* It was probably a borrowed copy, and kept out of my hands as far as reading was concerned, but I knew its pictures by heart and it helps to date this period. It was in 1895. Tree and Dorothy Baird had had a sensational success with the play in London, and were coming to Dublin. Dublin buzzed with talk of the book and the play. Svengali glared at us from all the

hoardings, and then came the news that the Gaiety Theatre book-
ing office, located beyond the counters in Cramer's spacious
music shop—a Venetian-Gothic palace in Westmoreland Street—
had been swept away in a swirl of ticket seekers. That was in
1895, when pantomime was all I knew of the theatre, but the
buzz reached the ears of the twelve-year-old who knew the shop
where his piano pieces came from.

That bookcase of my father's was in its little way a period piece,
as well as being in character with himself. It bore traces of that
typical Victorian product—Lubbock's *Best Hundred Books.*
Macchiavelli's *Prince* was there in a Routledge edition provoked
by Lubbock, but there were few of the consecrated English idols.
His Morley's *Walpole,* Lord Rosebery's *Pitt,* Frederick Harrison's
Cromwell and Mrs Green's *Henry II* came, I have no doubt, from
his own interest in political history, but it was an interest stimul-
ated by the new popularity won by Macmillan's new series of
such monographs. These, but more especially the long series of
the *English Men of Letters,* were typical of our later college reading, but for the moment my attention was more engaged with the
lively illustrations in *Don Quixote* and *Gil Blas* and not by any
grown-up literature. W. T. Stead's *Review of Reviews* came into
the house every month from its first issue in 1890. Reading it
was of course out of the question, but its pictures made a permanent lodgment. General Booth of the Salvation Army,
Parnell, Bismarck and Tolstoi, Madame Blavatsky and Marie
Bashkirtseff—their presence gave rise over the years to intermin-
able questioning and their importance was explained or dexter-
ously side-tracked until they lay for the time being quiescent in
the rag-bag of my mind.

My own bookstore began with my mother and it had two
well-defined sections. The toy age having passed and my father
evidently taking responsibility for footballs, cricket bats and
bicycles, my mother at Christmas and birthdays would produce
for us two volumes of Jules Verne and two others from Duffy's

National Library, never making any further difference between us than that the *Geburtstagskind* had first choice, and so our bookshelves grew. Jules Verne's store was inexhaustible. His books outpaced and displaced Henty and Ballantyne. They went beyond the adventures of Captain Nemo and Phineas Fogg, who have since had glorious reincarnations. We boarded the *Floating City*, the giant ship known as the *Great Eastern* whose planks we had already trod; made exotic journeys up the Amazon or with Michael Strogoff across the Russian steppes, or followed trails of history ending in the *Archipelago on Fire* in the Greek War of Independence.

Side by side with these sprouted the little green and gold volumes of Duffy's National Library. Sixteen of them arrived on my shelves. Monographs written for a national purpose by the writers of *The Nation* in the eighteen forties, D'Arcy Magee, Madden, MacNevin and the rest, they made hard going on first acquaintance. Just as the doings in the Château d'If were all that mattered to me in *The Count of Monte Cristo*, so also I willingly laid down John Mitchel's *Hugh O'Neill* after the battles of Clontibret and the Yellow Ford. I shied away from the final disaster at Kinsale, but loved the romantic and victorious encounter of O'Neill and Segrave at Clontibret when the opposing leaders rode out for single combat, their troops awaiting the shock of lance and horse to the final, fatal struggle, and Mitchel's invocation which I recognized from a school text:

> Now, gallant Saxon! hold thine own—
> No maiden's arms are round thee thrown.

But there was easier picking for me in Gavan Duffy's *Ballad Poetry of Ireland*, and in Thomas Davis, whose essays had become the Bible of Irish nationalism.

I dwell on this crop of '48 literature, not because it made part of my youthful reading, but because like *The Spirit of the Nation* and

Moore's *Melodies,* Gavan Duffy and Davis were general provender for the youth of my generation. I notice that in my edition of Gavan Duffy's *Ballads*—the forty-second—the author observes that in 1845 its three earlier editions were exhausted in less than a month, and in the sixth edition (1846) the publisher proudly notes that the book has had a larger circulation than any book published in Ireland since the Union. I should think that this record was later exceeded only by A. M. Sullivan's *The Story of Ireland* and perhaps by the *Irish Penny Readings*. All these filled the gap so obviously left by our wary government education boards and were in the hands of all outside the Establishment. The more militant amongst them had also Mitchel's *Jail Journal* and Sullivan's *Speeches from the Dock*. These were the books which lay at the roots of the new political groupings of my youth. They had a national appeal independent of the land question, and captured the urban population. Like Mazzini and *Italia Giovane* this literature of Young Ireland made up the gospel that Arthur Griffith and William Rooney were beginning to preach in Dublin in the 'little societies' which Yeats, at a middle period, chose to decry. Yeats, animated by his own high purpose and not without a certain early antagonism to Gavan Duffy whom he had not unreasonably conceived to stand in his way, found this literature altogether too rhetorical and too exclusively propagandist. Without it, however, he would not have found his first footing.

I have grossly anticipated the years. I must return to the age of leading strings and to those recurrent joys that distinguished the seasons and by which my parents introduced me to the outside world.

Earliest amongst them the Gaiety pantomime never lost its attraction. Once a year the family piled into a cab and rattled over the 'half-sets' to the magical chiaroscuro outside the theatre where bare-footed urchins were selling their broadsheets with 'all the pantomime songs one penny'. This was the vestibule of paradise. Already at mid-summer we hungrily looked out for the announcement of its name and the long accounts in the *Freeman's Journal* of the glories to come; of busy scene-painters and stage-carpenters in preparation, and of Mrs Gunn and her army of needle-women already at work on the costumes. We hoped the lot would fall on Sinbad or Robinson Crusoe, wrecked ships, rafts and desert islands. Incongruously La Loie Fuller might also be there dancing her flame dance, limelit in multi-coloured draperies, a miracle of colour. The vision did not hide Lauri, the Pantomime Cat or the funny man George Graves, all leading up to the ever more splendid kaleidoscope of the transformation scene, veil after ethereal veil lifting to disclose the triumphal entry and parade of the entire company. The harlequinade followed. We saw, though we did not know it, the last days of what once had been beginning and end of pantomime; we neither understood nor approved the conduct of so many of the audience who began to stand up between us and our view of the stage foolishly to adjust their wraps, as if they did not know that the best, or nearly the best, was still to come, with glittering Harlequin and Columbine, the pantaloon and strings and strings of sausages.

After St Patrick's Day came the family's regular visit to the Royal Hibernian Academy in Abbey Street—an impressive entertainment, but not to be compared with Pepper's Ghost and Vesuvius in eruption at Poole's Myorama in the Rotunda, nor even with what the National Museum had to offer. There we were let loose freely to wander and wonder at the magnificence of Lord Clare's coach and the yet more splendid coach of the Lord Mayor, and then to pick out the curiosities of the Bayeux tapestry which hung in replica in a now abolished corridor. It led to our last delight as with expected terror we passed under the belly of a suspended whale, into the natural history section, vicious sharks in attendance, and birds, to where in its isolated glory our Irish elk stood with far branching horns.

These things filled one's eyes in satisfactory measure, and could be collated with half understood books at home. So too, with regular opera-going which began when I was learning the piano. I was not, I fear, a diligent student, and at my practice time would be caught out reading a favourite book on the music-stand while making runs on the key-board which I thought might at a distance be taken for scales. But my parents were indulgent, and as a reward for more carefully executed selections from *La Sonnambula* or *Il Trovatore* they would bring me to an even better performance. Here also I was puzzled not a little. Not merely by an unintelligible plot, but by the plain fact that my *Selections* began with some light aria or waltz and invariably ended with the grand march. But the Ronsby or Moody Manners people playing in the vanished Leinster Hall arranged things otherwise, and I was left at sea waiting for my favourite tunes to appear in their right order.

To make up for this bad management there was the gallery singing. In the intervals of grand opera, whether in the Gaiety or the Leinster Hall, or in the Royal which replaced it, and from opposite sides of the gallery, 'Mr Byrne's song' or 'Mr O'Toole's song, please' was called for, and choice singers of Dublin's clans obliged in turn with 'The Heart Bowed Down' or 'I Dreamt that I Dwelt'. It was a Dublin tradition that Carl Rosa picked out William Dever one such night and added him to his company. At any rate, woe betide the stage manager who attempted to raise the curtain before the local repertoire was exhausted. These voices are now still, and with them this gallery singing, and most of a group of university students, who much later were heard from the Gaiety gallery at the Irish Literary Theatre's season in 1901. Between An Chraoibhín's (Douglas Hyde's) 'Casadh an t-Súgáin' and the Yeats-George Moore 'Diarmuid and Gráinne', Seamus Clandillon sang 'Fáinne Geal an Lae' and we supported him in chorus in 'Go Máiridh ár nGaedhilge Slán'. That was the first time songs in Irish were heard from a Dublin theatre gallery.

Family talk cleared up much of my confused reading and linked

49

D

actuality with history. Though the Parnell split might be tactfully avoided, the talk I listened to ran chiefly on the land agitation and the prospects of Home Rule. These vital issues engrossed everyone's attention. My mother was a farmer's daughter. With her passionate and retentive memory, before my schooldays were over there was little or nothing I had not learned from her of the iniquitous land system that prevailed in her parents' day and in her own youth. Coming of a long-lived stock and herself in due course an octogenarian, her memory to the end lost nothing of what she had heard or seen, and her recitals were in the plainest black and white—or, since she was an Ulster woman, should one rather say orange and green? She had little time for books, though it should also be said that a family connection and namesake McGahan was once a well-known traveller and correspondent, and had a statue erected to him in Sofia in recognition of his efforts on behalf of Bulgarian education. I was told he awakened Gladstone's conscience in the days of the Bulgarian atrocities as earlier Byron aroused Europe against the Turks and was similarly rewarded by his statue in Athens.

My father, as I have already suggested, was more historically minded and less agrarian. Though a Dublin man, his early schooling was in Mallow in the company of William O'Brien and Canon Sheehan, the one a Land Leaguer and Member of Parliament, the other the novelist whom I was later to meet, finding this friend of Judge Wendell Holmes a sad and, as I thought, a disillusioned man, but none the less eager to know what the young men of my generation were thinking about. With them at school was the more dubious figure whom I was to know as Sergeant Moriarty and later a Lord Justice in the old Court of Appeal.

My father laid claim to no such distinctions—nothing more than a bronze medal for third place in these islands in some technical examination in the South Kensington examinations. He was merely a technician in the telegraph service where my mother told me he invented some improvement in apparatus which was quietly adopted, but without any recompense.

He was a modest, companionable man, a pioneer cyclist who knew the roads of Ireland, loving both the open air and the workshop—our favourite playroom—he had fitted up for himself at home. He was our elder brother and shared with us his activities and information. Neither was inconsiderable. Journalistic contacts in the old *Freeman's Journal* made him familiar with the background of Irish politics. This and his liking for history and opera made the staple of his talk. Of himself he spoke not at all, and what personal details I knew of himself or his forebears I had almost wholly from my mother. He had not her genealogical turn and so I do not know for certain his exact relationship with Cardinal Cullen as claimed by an uncle. It was from my mother I first heard a story concerning another contemporary who was no friend of the Cardinal's. In my young days and in my father's company I often noticed certain oldish men, bearded and wearing slouch hats when silk hats were the common fashion. Like the Garibaldians and the followers of Mazzini who on principle wore soft black hats when Italy was under Austrian or Bourbon rule, these men followed an American army style. My father told me they were old Fenians. Now my father was a Home Ruler like the majority of people who had lived through the Land League and Parnellite days. The Fenian movement was discredited since its failure in 1867, and the general opprobrium incurred by the Invincibles—the irregular breakaway group—added further to this discredit. Yet I noticed that my father would speak with respect of these antique figures of the original brotherhood and distinguished them carefully from the Invincible group, a distinction no longer so carefully observed. It puzzled me to know why an orthodox supporter of Parnell and a friend of William O'Brien should so respect their political adversaries. My mother let that cat out of the bag. When my father was seventeen and living with his family, an elder brother, a universal favourite, was regarded particularly by my grandfather as the good boy of the family. One evening a cab drew up to the house and enquiry was made for 'Mr Curran'. My grandfather came to meet the visitor, and found himself confronted by James Stephens who had escaped from Richmond Gaol shortly before and was still 'on the run'. Both parties were equally surprised, for Stephens had business with the good boy of the family whose Fenian connection was quite unknown to his loving parent.

Before his marriage my father had been living in Queen's Square, situated within easy range of three theatres, the old Royal (later the Leinster Hall) the Gaiety and the Queen's and even closer to the Antient Concert Rooms. Queen's Square was a sort of tranquil Bohemia. It was at any rate the only area in Dublin that could properly be called an artists' quarter. Sculptors like Constantine Panormo, Edward Smyth's pupil, had lived there and the sculptors, and stone cutters' yards—Smith's, Harrison's and Pearse's—were close at hand. About the square lived many professors of music and elocution. It was the permanent residence of our stock companies, and many of the opera singers of Mapleson's famous company or the old Carl Rosa put up there, and their principals used to sing on Sunday mornings at Westland Row Church around the corner. In my father's young days touring companies were invading the home ground, and though the music teachers long held their ground against the Tooles and Irvings, the little square in large part was given over to theatrical lodgings. My father was himself no musician save for a life-long flirtation with the concertina. But tradition hung about the place, and my father had all the old stories of Boucicault melodrama in the Queen's and of opera in the old Theatre Royal before the Gunns built the Gaiety. He could speak of Giulini, the famous tenor, once the victim of his own popularity. Returning to the Gresham, his admirers triumphantly placed him on the open steps which then surrounded Nelson's Pillar, and he had to make a speech in his broken English assuring the crowd that he loved them very much, only later to find that his gold watch had been pinched by a questionable devotee.

Inevitably the classic stories of Titiens came out; the great soprano was the favourite of Dublin which she knew well for twelve or fifteen years. On every occasion 'The Last Rose of Summer' had to be sung. Once, the gallery held up the opera when the conductor, not knowing his Moore or 'Martha', a piano was dragged out from the wings. It toppled ingloriously into the footlights before the song could be sung. Most familiar was the story excelling Sir Walter Raleigh, when her carriage was unyoked after her performance of *Oberon* and the great diva was drawn by cheering young men to her hotel. It was a wet night, and they threw their coats down for Titiens to walk over them into the Shelbourne, and then waited until she sang them goodnight with 'The Last Rose'.

Queen's Square was therefore, I take it, one of the distant springs of our home talk. The theatre, music and politics were, I think, fairly characteristic of the houses I first knew.

Card games were for the young people; I remember little serious cardplaying. A little 'Twenty-five' or 'Spoil Five'; but Bridge or Poker had not come in to blanket talk. The card table was easily pushed aside for talk and music and for what the sideboard offered. On Sundays evenings, musical parties were general, to which guests brought their 'piece' and rivalled their favourite professional. Visitors dropped in freely and unannounced, and I soon found that whatever was missing from our domestic talk was amply supplied from two other sources.

I have said my father was a companionable man, but a certain shyness held him back from any exuberance. He was a good listener; else he had to be coaxed. Two of our old friends needed no such prompting; they gave tongue easily. Their talk flowed out like Clarence Mangan's rushing river and it afforded me Pisgah sight of two very different worlds. One was Edward Monks, father of my school friend, the late City Treasurer. He was born a year earlier but had the same birthday as George Bernard Shaw living next door to him in Synge Street. Shaw wrote to him on his eightieth birthday congratulating him on having been once twice his age. He was an old printer, father of his chapel in the *Freeman's Journal*. His talk ran easily on old Dublin music halls. They were a man's world of which I knew nothing.

I had never been inside Dan Lowry's, later the Olympia, until my father brought me there to see the first movie picture shown in Dublin. Kinematograph, cinematoscope, bioscope, its name was not yet agreed upon, and the projector did not seem very much larger in diameter than our own magic lantern. But lively little figures scurried up and down railway platforms to catch puffing trains, or hurried across London squares, all in a continual fall of snow. It interested my father—me too—but not much more than Ugo Biondi, the quick-change artist, and another talented but crippled performer who mounted an easel on the stage and painted pictures with his feet. Most thrilling to me was the fact that this was my first visit to a music hall.

Edward Monks could talk of Dan Lowry's in Crampton Court, and of the great MacDermott in the Grafton, and of Pat Kinsella's The Harp in Adam Court, and much of Ashcroft, 'The Solid Man', a near contemporary who sang in the Grafton. His songs were sung and whistled about the streets in my time:

> She wakes me up in the morning,
> Calling the hour of six.
> I'd the deuce of a race
> To get to the place
> For work at carrying bricks.

and another favourite, telling of a Dublin flittin':

> McGovern carried the crockery ware,
> The cradle was handed to me;

Murphy sat on top of the cart
Houldin' the clock on his knee.
The horse set off at a funeral trot,
He was staggering under his load.
He had great staying powers,
But it took him three hours
To travel a mile of the road.

Then there was the famous Val Vousden whom all of us knew—
not at the music halls where no lady went, but in pantomime or
more regularly at the Antient Concert Rooms. His family name
was Nugent and he was as versatile a performer as even Percy
French, though on a different level. He was Dublin's general
favourite in variety as an all-round one-man entertainer. One
such entertainment was 'The Rosicrusians', but he won greater
fame as polynational mimic in his 'Unity of Nations'. For both
he wrote the entire words and music, and sang, danced and acted
all the parts. He had a long working life, and its ups and downs.
My friend, the beloved Jimmy Montgomery, told me of him
breaking bottles and glasses at the bar of Kingsley's (predecessor
of Corless, in turn predecessor of Jammet's) by pelting them
with gold sovereigns. But Pat Kinsella who played in his
establishment with him as joint comedian had also had occasion
to release Val Vousden's teeth from a pawn-shop, and Joyce told
me that he last saw the old man being tenderly lifted into the
Black Maria at Green Street Courthouse.

Mr Monks rambled on in this way through old free-and-easies
earlier than the Mechanics, coeval for all I knew with the Talking
Fish and the penny gaffs in Capel Street. Capel Street then caught
and for long held my attention. Before Sackville Street or old
Carlisle Bridge was built it was the chief north side Dublin
artery leading to the Exchange and the Castle. Miss Sarah Purser
in her eighties could tell me of her aunt's house there in the
eighteenth century, where the chandeliers were taken down to be

cleaned for the opening of the parliament season—Grattan's parliament, *bien entendu*. Now a business street, I knew it first when brought by my father to buy my first and only violin, a Perry, small sized, but a late work of that distinguished Dublin violin maker, as its eighteenth–century label showed. That was in the shop of the MacNeill brothers, well known to every Dublin musician. There, too, in Capel Street as a small boy I had much truck with our first municipal lending library housed in a tall dingy house. For a librarian, the head of the City Library seemed to me a singularly cross-grained old fellow who sat apart unless his friend John Stanislaus Joyce came in to pass the time of day. Nor could the stalwart Michael Cusack, founder of the Gaelic Athletic Association, be lightly ignored. He banged the counter with his formidable blackthorn, and the dents it made remained long his memorial.

So music, literature and merchandise struggled for possession of this busy street. I knew it best from youthful raids on the library for Stevenson and Rider Haggard, Kipling, Marion Crawford and Seton Merriman, but happily also from frequent visits to the house there of a well-known musical family who play a part in Joyce's *Dubliners*. I had later to know its old association when ransacking the few surviving shops where sheet music was sold. That was in the 'thirties to satisfy Joyce's urgent demands for old pantomime libretti, and for the songs of Ashcroft, Horace Wheatley and Val Vousden. Fragments of them are embedded in *Finnegans Wake*, but the penny gaffs have disappeared from the neighbourhood, melted away like the Waxworks, and the Talking Fish is mute.

Those free-and-easies developed into something more concerto, but I still have some dim, perhaps mistaken, recollection of one in the old Star and Garter in Amiens Street. A schoolboy then, I did not venture in. I was going, on the invitation of an older lad, to an upper room to hear him in a debate on the French Revolution. I thought his exordium fine, '*a* French Revolution was justifiable, *the* French Revolution was not justifiable'. That was at the meeting of the New Ireland Literary Society, and its President was P. H. Pearse whom I then saw for the first time—a black-coated, serious, quiet-mannered youth whom I was later to know well.

If Monks gossiped of music halls, the talk of our second engaging visitor was on a less accessible level. He was the Librarian of the Royal Irish Academy, and his wife was the daughter of O'Longan, the last of the Irish Scribes, and an insufficiently recognized worker in the field of Irish scholarship. Old J. J. McSweeney's talk ran on O'Curry and O'Donovan, Petrie and Gilbert, the first three of whom lived and worked close to where I was born. The O'Longans indeed lived in my street, as also for a time did Edmund O'Donovan, the adventurous son of the antiquarian. My father knew him, but his stories of him were of his travels in the Near East, and of his pistol shooting from his bedroom window close to our own. The learned world of the Academy was as far from my ken as the music halls. True, O'Curry's *Mss. Materials* was in my father's bookcase, but still to me unintelligible. Listening to the talk of my elders, the Academy seemed a strange community of great and respected scholars, torn none the less by feuds and jealous rivalries. I was yet to learn that the immortals are not free from such rages and that however conspicuous these may be in the narrow compass of Irish scholarship, they are no unique phenomena in academies and institutes of learning. In a classic passage in the preface of his *Silva Gadelica* Standish Hayes O'Grady, an admitted master, has surveyed this battle area where 'the omniscient impeccable leviathans of science that headlong sound the linguistic ocean to its most horrid depths, and (in the intervals of ramming each other) ply their flukes on such audacious small fry as even on the mere surface will venture within their danger'.

In those days the Academy Library had no catalogue, but J. J. carried its index in his all-remembering brain. O'Grady paid tribute to the alacrity and accuracy of his answers to queries. For my part, for many years I heard only his gossip at home about O'Grady's lordly cetaceans of philology, collating it with the other harmonies of opera and music hall. Presently I could add and hold the picture of him sitting in his slippers at the Academy fire, his boots on the fender, opposite him Father Dinneen, the lexicographer and editor of the Munster poets, the old man's talk still running on.

3   Interlude, 1897-1898

THE Intermediate Education Board had so arranged its curriculum that a youngster who got a high place in its lower
grade examinations skipped a year and went straight on to the
next grade. Such a student might well find himself too immature
to enter the University. That was my case. My sensible parents
called a halt when I was fourteen and interpolated an agreeable
sort of sabbatical year during which, while remaining at school,
I had no examination to face, but could indulge a more liberal
taste. They sent me to the Academy of Music to learn the violin,
and the school authorities sent me with others for an hour or so
each week to the School of Art.

This intermezzo meant more to me than class work. It opened
up to me the south side of the city—*terra incognita* except for the
ducks in Stephen's Green and the show cases in the Museum.
Carrying my violin case down Brunswick Street (now Pearse

Street) I got to know the stone-cutters' workshops and Pearse's—
where, amongst others, Willie Pearse was learning his trade
alongside my friends Albert Power and Laurence Campbell—
past Smith's, and the scarcely remembered site of the activities of
the versatile and eccentric brothers McAnaspie. They were stucco
men, the more distinguished of the two being also a vigorous
controversialist on every conceivable topic. Their allegorical
figures and ornaments used to be in Fishamble Street and Copper
Alley and I suspect that a great figure of Esculapius with his
knotted club that was on Graham's in Westmoreland Street came
from their Brunswick Street premises. More remarkable were
several colossal busts that distinguished the façade of Butler's
Medical Hall in O'Connell Street near the bridge. Esculapius
was in the centre, but Thomas McAnaspie was also there wearing
a civic wreath and tunic, until *H.M.S. Helga* bombarded them
all from their perches during the Easter Rising. His most remarkable design was never executed. It was his proposed testimonial
to Daniel O'Connell, not accepted by the Monument Committee. He printed its description, however, on a broadsheet
from which I quote a few, but only a few, words. The Testimonial
or Temple was to be in storeys, the whole surmounted by a
statue of O'Connell. The first storey was the People's Hall; the
second a Mechanics' Institute; the third a Library, the fourth a
Museum 'for the antiquities and reminiscences of Ireland' with
'galleries'; the fifth 'a dome to be an observatory and furnished
with microscopes and other mathematical instruments for visitors
taking a birdseye view of the city' and finally 'an esplanade
outside round the bottom, the dome to be surmounted with
Ross's telescopes for such visitors taking a naked view of the city,
bay and surrounding neighbourhood, as well as a rear view of the
statue of O'Connell'.

In Brunswick Street also was Harrison's, where there used to
be a little model of Hogan's. In one way or another, by question
and answer, I grew interested in the stonecutter's craft. I suppose

every Dublin schoolboy who had his eyes open loved the stone monkeys who, across the College Park, have been playing billiards for years about the windows of the Kildare Street Club.

One of the Harrisons told me his father had brought him as a boy to see this amusing work which he had done when working side by side with the O'Shea brothers. These O'Sheas, master craftsmen, had done admirable work under Benjamin Woodward's direction in the Engineering School in Trinity College, and were then brought by Woodward and Ruskin to carve on Acland's Museum in Oxford. Their Oxford work was not universally appreciated—the Acland-Ruskin Gothic initiative gave rise to violent controversy; the O'Sheas took a hand in the quarrel and satirized the dissident members of Convocation, petrifying them as monkeys, parrots and owls which, I believe, have unfortunately not survived. But Harrison learned the monkey business from them and, reincarnated in stone, his monkeys are still playing billiards.

The work of the O'Sheas is worth dwelling on a little further as part of the stones of Dublin in which I was beginning to take an interest. My father told me he had seen the O'Sheas at work carving their foliage directly from plants and flowers held in a tumbler beside them. Much later Stephen Gwynn gave me a similar account, which must have been in the way of becoming a Dublin legend. It is certainly confirmed by the character of their work on the porch of the Club, but more remarkably by the carving in the vestibule and hall within. Here one can see, on the jambs of an arch, dragon flies, lizard, weasel, squirrel and frog, and capitals of pillars wrought with such water motifs as reeds, water lilies and ducks. Small wonder that Ruskin wrote to Acland gleefully hailing the success of this new faith in nature and in the genius of the unaided workman who gathered from the fields the materials he needed.

So, telescoping the years, I reached my music lesson at the Academy where my master was Paddy Delany, a pupil of

Secvic. He was a brilliant performer on the instrument to which he was fanatically devoted, but we did not take our lessons too seriously. He knew I was a fly-by-day, but he liked talking French; he spoke of Sarasate and the one or two other celebrities who passed through town. I admired my master's exemplary virtuosity, attained the sixth position on my fiddle, played at least Handel's *Largo* and Gounod's *Ave Maria,* and learned to love the violinist's art.

As to the School of Art, it was a dead waste of time spent in drawing cones and cubes and shading with charcoal and stump. But the school was fortunately situated between the National Gallery and the National Library, with no locked gate to block, as now, the passage between. I grew intimate with both. I must indeed have been brought to the National Gallery on some earlier visitation, for two pictures, and two pictures only, were already in my mind. One was Maclise's *Marriage of Eva and Strongbow.* It might well have appeared in the long list of historical subjects drawn up by Thomas Davis for the attention of our native artists—a list indicative of the taste of Davis's period, and Prince Albert's. It imposed itself by reason of its size and subject, a marriage ceremony conducted on a battlefield amidst the heaped corpses of combatants outside the walls of ruined Waterford. I am more proud of the eclectic taste that anchored me before the small canvas of Rembrandt's *Flight into Egypt*, a little nightpiece well designed to fascinate a schoolboy by its mystery of firelight, water and cave. The National Gallery has since been enriched by many other fortunate acquisitions, but it was those two incongruous canvases that awakened in me a new sense.

Once a year my parents had accustomed me to the Royal Hibernian Academy in Abbey Street—a dutiful treat. Nearly half the exhibitors there were English, and the painters to whom reverence was paid were Alma Tadema, Lord Leighton and Sir Edward Poynter. There were also a few of our own—Hone, Osborne and Vincent Duffy; an occasional Yeats, father and son and portraits by Sarah Purser of people who, I understand, were interesting. Soon I could go by myself and made friends with the Keeper of the Academy, Vincent Duffy, of whom I must always speak with love and respect. He would take me round the pictures. He took no account of the great names of Tadema or Leighton. He would pass them over with a twinkle in his eye, but whenever we passed a good painting by anyone worth while, he would halt and direct my attention to it. He himself had begun many years before as a painter, somewhat in the manner of James Arthur O'Connor, but with a vein of poetry in his work that was all his own and a predilection for certain subjects which gave him the nickname of 'Moonlight Duffy'. When I knew him he had veered towards impressionism too early for the public taste, and so he remained unvalued and unbought. One year, George Russell (AE) told me he showed a large landscape which AE particularly admired. When the exhibition closed, the picture unsold, AE went to Duffy's studio to study it more closely. He found that the painter had scraped off his landscape and was at work on a new composition on the same canvas; he could not afford to buy a new one. The second picture, inferior to the first, AE said, is now in one of our galleries. I saw Duffy in his last days in the Richmond Hospital, his bed near a window, and my last recollection of this lovable old man is of him sitting up in bed to describe for me and paint in gesture the moon which he had seen behind the trees the night before.

Now, rising fifteen, I ventured into the National Library and, without the usual formality of introduction and reader's ticket, became a regular reader. This was due to a chance conjecture. At home I had got to know something of John Mitchel and the '48 writers. I had also been reading the Christmas number of *Pearson's Magazine* which found its way that year into our house. In it was Shelley's 'Ode to the West Wind', elaborately fitted up with coloured marginal illustrations. Shelley's verse thrilled me, but I was no less excited by an article by a certain Mrs Gallup, hot gospeller of the Baconian theory. It plainly made nonsense of Shaw's *History of English Literature,* my school textbook. The article devoted particular attention to Ignatius Donnelly's *The Great Cryptogram,* but this book was not to be had in the Municipal Library. I was told it might be in the National Library. Fired by a double curiosity, and passing the steps of the National Library once or twice a week, I ventured in, mounted the shining staircase to the rotunda where garlanded cherubs circled in a frieze over the bowed heads of attentive readers. The assistant librarian, then, I think, that fine naturalist Robert Lloyd Praeger, was at his post at the counter, a stalwart Nordic, sturdy as an oak tree. I timidly enquired if he had Donnelly's *The Great Cryptogram* and the files of Mitchel's *United Irishman.* He looked dubiously at me, but with humorous eyes. He asked me my age and had I a reader's ticket. Presently, T. W. Lyster, the librarian, was quietly beside him and I found myself conducted to a chair at a table, and the two big red and gold volumes of *The Great Cryptogram* planted carefully in front of me. From one week to another I ploughed through them, and for eighteen months I was a passionate Baconian. Whenever the word Shakespeare occurred in my Shaw, the name of the pretentious Stratfordian was scored out and the rightful heir written in. Following Ignatius Donnelly, those never-sufficiently-to-be-praised librarians and their staff fetched out for me the bound file of the *United Irishman,* and after Mitchel its successor Fintan Lalor's *Irish Felon.* Mitchel's bitter rhetoric, Fintan Lalor's incisiveness, made their inevitable impression, and most of all the handling of those old files brought the sense of actuality which contact with original sources can bring to the student, however young. Ignatius Donnelly's and Mrs Gallup's theories faded away, leaving behind some shadowy enlarged acquaintance with Tudors and Jacobeans. The writings of the '48 men of letters and their controversies might remain subject for debate, but the sense of actuality grew more vivid. Outside the library the streets were astir with demonstrations and counter-demonstrations. The suppressed papers of Mitchel and Lalor found their successor in Arthur Griffith's *United Irishman*—the years were 1897 and 1898, the years of Queen Victoria's Diamond Jubilee and the centenary of the '98 Insurrection.

A new turbulence agitated the city centre. Hitherto political manifestations took place at its outskirts. The schoolboy, pushing his way through crowds assembled near the polo-ground in the Phoenix Park, grew familiar with the torrential oratory and vehement gestures of William O'Brien, and the somewhat more restrained prophetic denunciations and appeals of John Dillon, or, indoors, there were the more orderly assemblies in the Rotunda or Mansion House. These were the meeting-places of the well-known parliamentary leaders and the chiefs of the National League, and from 1898 of the United Irish League. In what club, conventicle or Orange hall the Unionists met was of no general concern. They were the established ascendancy indifferent to the populace, manifest at rare intervals with army and police when some Lord Lieutenant might be arriving or departing. With the Queen's Jubilee came a change. The city was beflagged with Union Jacks; the fashionable shops, known to enjoy viceregal patronage by the royal arms displayed on their fronts, had special decorations with monograms and mottoes conspicuously mounted, and at night all were brilliantly illuminated. Special trains brought every loyalist in the country up to see the city lights, and the crowds which filled the streets were plain evidence to *The Times, The Irish Times* and *The Daily Express* that the loyalty of the Irish people to the crown had been grossly misrepresented. It is true that when evening fell and the average Dublin citizen was free from work, nightly affrays took place between them and the Trinity boys; stones would fly, illuminated windows crash, and in memory I see a schoolboy swept to shelter by a charge of mounted police. This was of no more significance than the doings of a rabble egged on by a few scribblers and

E

agitators, whose nightly sally port was 32 Lower Abbey Street, the headquarters of a certain Celtic Literary Society—its chiefs two young men called William Rooney, and a compositor, Arthur Griffith. This Jubilee business was local and lasted only a week or so, but the '98 celebration was general and more prolonged. Supplements on '98 appeared in the national papers; memories of '98 were revived; fife and drum bands appeared at '98 meetings all over the country; songs like 'A Nation Once Again' were heard once more, and Ingram's 'Who Fears to Speak of '98' for a time replaced 'God Save Ireland' as the national anthem. It was in that year I saw for the first time the striking figure of Maud Gonne when she was addressing a crowd at the Custom House. She passed through the country like an angel of revolution, and passed, I may add, into folk history. Folk history takes little account of time. With the confused memory of age an old Mayo man told a friend of mine that she was the sister of General Humbert who landed at Killala in 1798.

The celebrations culminated in a great meeting at Stephen's Green, an anti-climax as it turned out, for we laid the foundation stone there at the top of Grafton Street of a statue of Wolfe Tone, and ingloriously went no further with the work until the 1960s. More complete '98 memorials sprouted about the country—many deplorable, a few passable, none more excellent than Oliver Sheppard's two admirable works in the Bull Ring in Wexford, and in Wicklow.

In the following two years our political passion was further heightened by the events of the Boer War and the ill-conceived visit of Queen Victoria, which some misguided authority thought would stimulate recruiting in Ireland. She had as little affection for this country as we had for the 'Famine Queen' but her appearance here aroused more pity than dislike—a sullen, drowsy, hardly conscious figure, mechanically tilted in her carriage seat, as we understood, to acknowledge what salutations greeted her. Salutations there were, to be sure, because the same concentration of officials and scattered loyalists lined a few principal streets.[1] So also there were nightly demonstrations by the same Dublin artisans who came out with hostile intent, cheering for the Boers, challenging the 'college boys', smashing illuminations. Through the crowd—near Stephen's Green and in Dame Street—twice I had glimpse of an ass and cart with a shrouded coffin labelled *The Famine Queen.* Ass, cart and coffin kept bobbing up here and there like the sandwich men in *Ulysses,* or like Bloom's throwaway on the changing tide of Joyce's Anna Livia. Further out, in a respectable suburb, over the roof of Maud Gonne's house, and until the police laid successful siege to it, there hung for hours at half-mast a black silk petticoat. Qualify these happenings as you may—disloyal, unchivalrous, mirth-making or ridiculous—they represented plainly to me the true feelings of the Dublin artisan in the years of the Diamond Jubilee and the Boer War. They are not gainsaid by the Dublin Fusiliers who were carried aboard at the North Wall for South Africa, cheering for Kruger and the Boers.

This was also the moment chosen by Trinity College to confer an honorary degree of its University upon Joseph Chamberlain, wrecker of Gladstone's Home Rule Bill, friend of Captain O'Shea, and the man who, in popular opinion, used the fiasco of the *Times*-Pigott forgeries to trigger off the O'Shea-Parnell divorce case. It was an ill-chosen moment, the week of Colenso and Spion Kop. I quote Sir Edward Cadogan's account of the conferring:

> This was a wonderful scene in the great hall of Trinity College when Mr Chamberlain received his degree and had expressed his gratitude with his unfailing eloquence. His reception by the students, whose loyalty had always been

1. I am reminded of the women who sailed out from Cody's Lane (now Botanic Avenue) to meet the Queen on an unexpected afternoon visit. They ran after her carriage with the warning 'Look out, ma'm, the Boers are coming!'

proverbial, was overwhelming. By way of comic relief the students had torn down the flag over the Mansion House. If I remember rightly, the device upon it was an Irish harp uncrowned, and they deposited it upon the floor so that Mr Chamberlain could not fail to tread it underfoot.[2]

This was, of course, at an hour when people were at work, but in the afternoon, when the news got around the town, College Green filled with an angry crowd. Not until the labour disturbances in 1913 did I see a Dublin crowd so dangerous. By a back gate and devious route Mr Chamberlain escaped the Liffey.

These students were bound to the Empire by every motive of self-interest and old loyalties, but those days, and this episode, stick in my mind rather as the last demonstrations in Dublin of the narrowing oligarchy and as the nadir of nineteenth-century Trinity College. In world affairs the Boer War represented the apex of the British ascendancy upon which this oligarchy depended. It was the last war fought by Britain without an ally, and Arthur Balfour once said that no empire can survive alone, without allies. It marked the end of an era. Hallam wrote of it that: 'No unbiased observer who derives pleasure from the welfare of his species can fail to consider the long and uninterruptedly increasing prosperity of England as the most beautiful phenomenon in the history of mankind.'[3]

I confess that to one biased observer Hallam's visionary phenomenon remains obscured by the passage through his streets of the symbolic coffin of the Famine Queen.

2. E. Cadogan, *Before the Deluge*, London 1961, 77.
3. H. Hallam, *View of the State of Europe during the Middle Ages*, London 1869, chapter 8.

4 The Old University College Staff

IN reviving the memory of Father Delany's first staff, I must
necessarily rely on what my elders told me but, curiously
enough, my own recollection goes back to one who was in the
original group appointed by Newman himself, and yet was one
of my own examiners. I mean, of course, Thomas Arnold.
Tommy Arnold, as we all called him, was Matthew Arnold's
brother, and held the earliest college chair in English literature.
At one time or another he edited Wycliffe, Clarendon and Addi-
son, and wrote a substantial manual of English literature to which
Gerard Manley Hopkins made a contribution. I encountered him
first at an early scholarship oral which he was conducting as a
Fellow of the Royal. I answered some questions he put regarding
the first campaign in the Parliamentary Wars in England, and
correctly enough made mention of Oxford and its neighbourhood. He asked me courteously was I ever there, and upon my

negative answer he opened up on the beauty of the Oxford countryside, through which I gladly led him on, my oral becoming an aural while his colleagues sat back smilingly. He was then a man of seventy-six or seven, but active enough to deliver formal addresses. His regular class work grew less in 1897, and ceased very shortly afterwards. I heard him lecture in the Aula Maxima in 1899 or 1900 on Anglo-Saxon poetry. I have forgotten what he said of Beowulf and Cynewulf, but I am not alone in remembering his clear thin utterance with its slight stammer, his tall figure stooped at the reading desk, and his clear-cut features with wide mouth, and the fringe of side whiskers which he wore in the fashion of men of his generation like the old Chief Baron Palles. We students understood that he was the original Philip Hewson of Clough's *Bothie of Tober na Vuolich*

> . . . Philip Hewson was a poet,
> Hewson a radical hot, hating lords and scorning ladies,
> Silent mostly, but often reviling in fire and fury
> Feudal tenures, mercantile lords, competition and bishops.

But as he himself said 'there was a dialectic force in Philip that certainly was never in me.' Of this we had no occasion to judge. Looking down on the Green from the windows of our English Literature class we used to see him every Saturday morning passing on his way from his house in Leeson Street to the University Church, and we watched with affectionate respect this old gentleman of varied religious experience who, we knew, had seen Wordsworth called to order at a meeting at Grasmere, held to protest against the proposed introduction of railways to the Lake District, and, in Wordsworth's own house at Rydal Mount, had heard him read a sonnet fresh from the poet's quill.

A greater literary figure than Arnold played a lesser part in college life in the late 'eighties. The President brought over

Gerard Manley Hopkins in 1883 to fill one of the two chairs in classical literature. He had passed from Balliol to Stonyhurst and taught Greek in our College until his death six years later. His pupils, but few others, understood he was a poet. He had published little, and that little obscurely, and was spoken of only as a shy, sensitive recluse.

I used to hear also how Hopkins was chaffed for his Englishness by his colleague, Père Mallac, a French lawyer and free-thinker who became Catholic and Jesuit, and belonged to the philosophy faculty in the College. These were days of Anglo-French tension, even before Fashoda. Hopkins in exile was all the more English, punctiliously observing English patriotic anniversaries. On a May morning, Mallac, walking with William Magennis in the garden of No. 86, met Gerard Hopkins wearing a peony in his buttonhole. Hopkins asked them why they also did not wear a flower on the Queen's birthday. Mallac stared into the peony and said, 'Yellow cauliflower.' Hopkins paled with indignation and retorted 'Lâche!' I imagine that behind the chaffing and politics or the outgoing of his heart to 'our redcoats, our tars', there lay the eternal feud between Platonist and Aristotelian. Hopkins leaned towards Plato and Duns Scotus, but the black-a-vised Mallac stood fiercely for the Stagirite. Anyway, the poet had a good friend in his fellow Oxonian, Father Darlington, who knew how to tempt the displaced recluse from his books to observant country walks, and when Gerard Hopkins wrote at that date as seeming a stranger amongst strangers, and of his remove to Ireland, it was to speak of Ireland also as a place where

> . . . I can
> Kind love both give and get.

Ten years later I scarcely heard his name mentioned in the College, and it was not until Robert Bridges brought out his poems in 1918 that people realized that a major poet had lived and died in their midst.

As large an oblivion on our part covered the lesser name of Father J. J. O'Carroll who was an exact contemporary of Hopkins in the College, and an unusual figure. Father Delany included him in his first staff, and he died in College in the same year as the poet. Master of seventeen languages and their literatures, he could speak eight others, and read in still eight or nine more. He wrote no book but contributed to the first monthly connected with University College, *The Lyceum*, both on early Irish history, but more substantially, and for those very early days, I should imagine startlingly—for this was in 1887—on Russian literature, ranging freely over unfamiliar steppes peopled by Zhukovsky and Batyushkov as over those by Pushkin, Gogol and Dostoievsky. He studied Middle Irish, wrote extensively on the Ossianic poems in the first two volumes of the *Gaelic Journal*, worked in the old Society for the Preservation of the Irish Language and in the Gaelic Union which followed it, and conducted a class in modern Irish in the College.

O'Curry's Chair in Newman's University was in Irish history and archaeology; O'Looney succeeded to it upon O'Curry's death in 1862. Precisely when it lapsed I do not know, but when Father Delany became President of the College the department was extended and entitled Irish Language, History, Archaeology, with three professors, Fathers O'Carroll, Denis Murphy, Edmund Hogan. Father Denis Murphy did little classwork in the College, and his once well-known *Cromwell in Ireland* and his *Aodh Ruadh O'Donnell* are now out-dated. Father Edmund Hogan, who became a Fellow of the Royal in 1889, is still an authority in Irish studies. He came well down into my day, and though I was not his pupil I had occasion to meet him frequently both out of doors and in his bed-sittingroom-study, and twice or three times he fell into the lens of my camera. Being then something of a valetudinarian he worked in front of a famous folding screen pasted with old *Weekly Freeman* political cartoons, and for the good of his health he kept a box of pills in his bedroom slippers, just as Sherlock Holmes kept his tobacco in his Persian pair. Dr Seamus O'Kelly, George Clancy and Seamus Clandillon made up his class in my degree year, and assisted him with the slips of his now indispensable *Onamasticon*.

A decade or so earlier his most distinguished pupils, John MacNeill and Charles MacNeill, served their scholars' apprenticeship with him on the spadework of *Cath Ruis na Rig*. John MacNeill was later invited by Father Delany to lecture in the College; it was in this course of lectures he made a modern and fruitful approach to the study of early Irish history. MacNeill has written finely on his old Bollandist master, the link between the old and the new in Irish scholarship, and the last of a long line who used Latin easily and naturally as the language of communication between the learned.

It goes against the grain to pass over with bare mention the brilliant group of scientists who, if they were not as picturesque as some of their literary colleagues, or as their predecessor John Casey, the mathematician, who demonstrated trigonometry sensibly with a raw potato, made a strong bony structure for the College. There were Harry McWeeney and Arthur Conway, F.R.S., in mathematics, Hugh Ryan in chemistry, and in physics the gifted and short-lived Thomas Preston with John McClelland, F.R.S., and Huston Stewart. Their influence was felt throughout the College and in the Academic Council, but not specializing in science I saw nothing of them in class except for Huston Stewart who lectured in the old Physics Theatre to a conjoint mob of us—first Arts and first Medicals. The curious in these matters may glimpse that class at a disrespectful moment in the *Portrait of an Artist*. Stewart was not the most distinguished of his Faculty, but my one year with him and science gave me a respect for both. The aptness and precision of his language, the conciseness of his definitions, the skilful economy of his experiments, the unaffected respect with which he quoted his authorities taught me the roots which science and arts have in common.

Two other notable figures of the old Catholic University staff were still active in my day. Dr Sigerson and Mgr Gerald Molloy were both scientists. Sigerson, of whom I shall write on a later page, had the chair of biology, Molloy of experimental physics, but apart from science they had little else in common except their wide culture and, if you like, their old-fashioned ways. Otherwise they lived on different planes. Like Tommy Arnold, Mgr Molloy had surrendered regular classwork—if he ever had any. He lived secluded from the rabble of students on the splendid drawing-room floor of No. 86 St Stephen's Green, still nominally Rector of the phantom Catholic University, but in effect rather less than caretaker. He belonged to the race of Castle Catholics; none of us cared for his politics, and this, perhaps unfairly, coloured our general opinion of him. He was a tall, courtly figure walking with a limp and a stick. I used to think Talleyrand must have looked like him. Occasionally he delivered public lectures in College, and with his unequalled talent for expounding in a popular way the most recent discoveries in physics, he was in great demand. Outside the College, or within, he drew large and satisfactory fashionable audiences. He enjoyed a special prestige by reason of his association with Marconi in exploring the aether. As students we loved his lecture performances, as he bent tentatively and most carefully over his bag of tricks. Invariably his first attempt was unsuccessful, and with the help of his lab. assistant, George Davenport, he adjusted a screw or two. The second attempt also failed—another screw was adjusted, and on the third trial he produced the waves he wanted, and sent them to ring a bell at the end of his long table, where George stood to receive them and the applause of the audience. We were not the less enthusiastic because we knew that George took the poorest view of a lecturer who brought off his experiment at the first go-off. The *houp-la* always should come with the third.

Father Delany's quality as educationalist comes out in his choice of these men. I exclude Mgr Molloy whom he inherited, and include his capacity to work with them smoothly. In 1901 he set up and shared the government of the College with an Academic Council of six professors—five of them laymen who were elected every three years by and from the teaching staff. At this period, and for years afterwards, Trinity College was still governed by the Provost with seven Senior Fellows who held office for life. Another significant advance made at this period was the admission of women students to the College lectures, or at least to the principal lectures which were delivered in the *Aula Maxima*. These and his development of the philosophy side of the College were fundamental changes, but otherwise the President's personal influence and contact with the students was small as compared with others on the staff, such as Father Tom Finlay, Father Darlington and William Magennis.

Finlay's name is indissolubly linked with the economics of our agriculture, but his influence on successive generations of students went far beyond that. This Cavan-born son of a Scots engineer had a closer knowledge of the Irish character, and a larger grasp of public affairs, than anyone else in the College. Brought up on the classics, his early training had been in France, and he came back a formidable logician gifted with style. In logic, political economy and political science he was more than competent, and what he had to say he said with authority, precision and a mordant wit. Walter Bagehot, his fellow economist, once divided men into molars and incisors. Father Tom was one of the incisors. His was the way of sharp definition and analysis. Popular slogans and the easy phrases of the platform shrivelled under his cool humorous dissection, curled up and died. At first contact he shocked my credulous youth, and he was a pain to platform politicians. But he was far from being the negative, corrosive-academic type. Whenever possible he directed the activities of his students into writing and into public affairs. One way of judging him is through the careers of his pupils; another is by reference to the monthlies which he founded and edited: *The*

Lyceum and *The New Ireland Review,* predecessors of *Studies.* His teaching career covered three generations of college students. The first included William Magennis, W. P. Coyne and Bob Donovan, who as post-graduates first shared in the management of *The Lyceum.* The second, my own contemporaries, Tom Kettle, Hugh Kennedy, Arthur Cleary, John Marcus O'Sullivan, Felix Hackett; the third, a notable proportion of the men who with some of their seniors staffed our government after the Anglo-Irish treaty. These varying types, philosophers, economists, men of letters and of law, had one common denominator, an unselfish instinct for public service. They got their impetus in great measure from Finlay and they had their baptism in ink in the papers Finlay founded, edited and in turn passed into their general control.

The first of these papers, the almost forgotten *Lyceum,* ran from 1887 to 1894. It was peculiarly sensitive to the atmosphere in which it was born, reflecting some of the strength, but more of the weakness, of its milieu. Conservative without being reactionary, its temper affected the quality of the college teaching even in my day. Seen with the hindsight of another century it can be both admired and smiled at. Its aim was to promote a Catholic solution of the educational and social problems which were pressing themselves, at home and abroad, on public attention, and within set limits it gallantly discharged this task. Its staff were all connected with the College, and as such their interests were primarily scholastic. Some of them were also concerned in outside journalism—on *The Nation* and *Freeman's Journal*—but engaged in education they were committed to treat their *Lyceum* themes not as politicians but in the tone and temper of theorists. They were expressly non-party and non-political. They had, therefore, to walk delicately. It is all the more intriguing to see how the Finlay brothers—for Father Tom had an able coadjutor in his brother Peter the theologian—tempered the tone of the theorist to the sharpest polemical edge. Father Tom had a free field in his surveys of Irish economics, as had his colleagues in some, but not all, educational issues. Karl Marx, Henry George and Mivart were frequent targets, and more transitory topics were found in theosophy and Masonry, for those were the days of Madame Blavatsky and Mrs Besant, of Nathan and the Grand Orient. In home affairs the pledge of total abstinence from party politics was studiously, even pedantically observed. Sir Charles Gavan Duffy might, indeed, write at large on the constitution of a hypothetical Irish Senate, but questions of Irish land tenure and taxation were discussed without any reference to the land agitation or Home Rule. From start to finish, that is to say from 1887 to 1894 over the period of the land agitation, the later Home Rule movement and throughout the Parnell 'split', the name of Parnell or of the Land League or National League, so far as I can see, does not occur in the paper. It is true that during the 'split' in 1892 and 1893 there are three articles of an expository character—I should think from the pen of Father Peter Finlay—on the relation of Church authority with politics. But that is all. In the issue following the death of Parnell there is no mention made of it, though space is found for an article on 'Dante as a Politician'. Such were the self-imposed limits within which *The Lyceum* was conducted.

As an organ of literary criticism it also suffered from the comparative vacuum which existed in Irish letters through most of the 'eighties and was only beginning to fill up. It printed no original literature to speak of. In this respect, even when the home fields were scanty, *The Lyceum* compares unfavourably with its contemporaries, Father Matt Russell's *Irish Monthly* or *The Dublin University Review,* that adventurous, independent and therefore short-lived monthly edited by T. W. Rolleston and Hubert Oldham who was later to be a professor in University College. Both these papers had the first fruits of the new poets, and *The Lyceum's* air of curule authority was no substitute for Father Matt Russell's judicious eye, as quick to discern the young shoots, presently to ripen to an abundant harvest, as to rebuke any occasional brash or unmannerly criticism. On the other hand, *The Lyceum* did show a sustained effort to keep abreast of current trends abroad in politics, science and letters, even though O'Carroll's studies of Russian and Scandinavian writers, including complimentary reference to Ibsen, degenerated in a later hand to a grotesque slating of *The Master Builder*. There were articles in plenty on European figures from Jacopone da Todi or Bruno to Zola, with much attention given to English and American writing—Tennyson, Arnold, Meredith, Pater, Whitman and Whittier. These articles, reflecting a general taste, are now period pieces as is all good journalism. They are donnish, well-informed, acute, over-refined and, at times, pernickety. They are avowedly polemical when literature was exalted to an ersatz-religion, and grandmotherly in their reaction from any approach to realism.

The Lyceum's rare excursions into art criticism were equally true to the reigning taste in paint. Those were the days when $4' \times 3'$ photogravures of Alma Tadema and Leighton spread themselves on the walls of our doctors' waiting-rooms, innocent of what the future held. Impressionism which had barely touched our shores was frowned on, and so when *The Lyceum's* art critic, W. P. Coyne, paid his visit to the Royal Hibernian Academy in 1889 he could praise Sir Frederick's 'masterly work exhibiting all the qualities of his beautiful and distinguished but mannered style' when Vincent Duffy's work 'is sometimes so roughly blocked as to be scarcely intelligible' and 'Mr Hone's seapieces are vigorous but rude even to the daubing point'. One may add that the Dublin University reviewer at the same date wrote down Rembrandt as often 'sordid and cynical'.

The Lyceum writers were on surer ground in scholarship. The scholars were the forerunners of the poets. The work, as it appeared in its gradual efflorescence, of Whitley Stokes, Standish Hayes O'Grady, D'Arbois de Jubainville, was cordially recognized, and when in 1893 Hyde's *Love Songs of Connacht* appeared in its modest form, this founding book of the literary revival was received with admirable discernment and praise. When without any break in time *The New Ireland Review* replaced *The Lyceum,* it sought and won a wider audience, supporting the new movements with outside contributors like MacNeill and Hyde who were giving a new direction to our affairs, and were themselves presently to be of the College staff.

I have dwelt on the character of the old *Lyceum*—observant and critical of new trends in literature, practical in analysis, cautious, and beyond measure reticent in domestic politics,— because enough of these traits survived in my early days to mark a good deal of college teaching. Not so the student body, which was neither cautious nor reticent. No discreet abstinence from politics was evident amongst them. They were eloquently divided between an orthodox majority, readers of the Home Rule *Freeman's Journal,* many of them sons of members of the Irish Parliamentary Party, and a small minority who read the insurgent *United Irishman* and preached the new doctrine of Arthur Griffith and William Rooney. A very few were members of the Celtic Literary Society, or the militant Dungannon Club, or the Confederates, but this handful of artsmen was fortified by a strong battalion of medicals from the Cecilia Street School ready to play an active part in any intra or extra commotion. The Gaelic League occupied a middle field with general respect.

On a different level the climate was determined by the men I have mentioned who at one time or another held between them the chairs of logic, metaphysics and ethics. In the early years of the Royal University its philosophy faculty had merited stringent criticism. The degree in this faculty was once stigmatized by Father Walter MacDonald of Maynooth as 'the easiest earned degree in Christendom'. The co-operation of Finlay, Magennis and Park, of Queen's, Belfast, changed all that, and from before my time the philosophy classes in University College were attracting a large proportion of the best brains in the College.

79

Father Darlington, who passed between this faculty and the English chair, was not the least active of its *vulgarisateurs*. As Dean of the College he knew all the students, was accessible to all, and zealous for their comfort. His mannerisms have become legendary: the brisk rubbing of hands and quick initial assentations— over-quick at times, as when W. P. Coyne is said to have told him of his impending marriage. 'Just the very thing, Mr Coyne, just the very thing. I was about to do the same myself.' In my time, as well as being Dean, he held the English chair before passing into the philosophy faculty. His teaching in each profited from his experience in the other. Perhaps he was not so very distinguished in either, but I found him stimulating. He was a full-blooded Aristotelian revelling in definitions and distinctions. His approach to Hamlet through Aristotle and Aquinas had for me a particular flavour as when in a characteristic excursion he attributed Hamlet's introspection, hesitations and dubiety to his Wittenberg training, in contrast with the decisive action of Laertes upon his return from the school of Paris. This Aristotelian undercurrent emerged whenever the Dean spoke, as he often did, in the College societies, and it fitted in well with Father Delany's dictum that the philosophy faculty should be the heart of any university. It was so in the University College I knew. None of us escaped its tincture. It coloured both our literature classes and our debates. The regular textbook in this course was Boedder's *Natural Theology,* one of the Stonyhurst series in Catholic philosophy. These manuals were in general circulation in the College, and very accessible. I retain still my Boedder and a copy of Rickaby's *General Metaphysics.* Neither my class-fellow Joyce nor myself followed any course in philosophy, but turning over their pages I read again with a new interest certain familiar Thomistic dicta; in Boedder a page of aesthetics enshrining *Pulchra dicuntur quae visa placent,* and in Rickaby a more extended treatment of the beautiful, turning upon definitions of Aquinas and the significance of the *integritas, consonantia* and *claritas,* which

80

were presently to occupy the mind of Stephen Daedalus. These books were in the hands of Joyce's class-fellows. He himself keener than the rest on his special objective and quicker to claim his property where he found it, found here the starting point of his aesthetics.

F

5 George Sigerson

D R Sigerson, whom I have mentioned as a contributor to *The Lyceum* in the 'eighties, wrote earlier in late issues of *The Atlantis,* the bulky and learned University periodical founded by Newman. He spent most of his long life in the medical schools of the Catholic University and University College, but the part this physician, biologist, historian and poet played in public life and in the literary movements of his day, as well as my own intimacy with him, make it impossible for me to confine my recollections to within college walls. My friendship with him began on a day when I was still not much more than a student, knowing him only from a distance. I waited upon him seeking a contribution for *St Stephen's,* the cheerful college paper I was then editing. Those were the days when Zimmer, 'the Tiger of Greifswald', held the field of Celtic studies in that University. Dr Sigerson gave me a contribution which established St Patrick as a Zimmerian sun-myth: a philological *jeu d'esprit, Das Lied von Sankt Patrick,* the original of the Dublin ballad incorporating an ancient race tradition:

> St Patrick was a gentleman
> He came of decent people,
> He built a church in Dublin town
> And on it placed a steeple
>
> etc.

or in Ur-Teutonic:

> Sankt Patrick war ein gentleman
> Und Kind rechtschaffner Leute
> Er baut ein Kirchlein in Dublin
> Mit Turm und mit Geläute.

> Sein Vater war ein Gallacher
> Seine Mutter eine Brady
> Sein Muhme 'ne O'Shaughnessy
> Und Base des O'Grady.

That meeting was my admittance to a life-long friendship which was for me an inexhaustible illumination. His talk was never profuse, but his mind was steeped in history, and enriched with wide experience of men and affairs. Touch him at any point and he had something relevant and fresh to say. At dinner one evening at his house, No. 3 Clare Street, one of the guests, Professor Mary Hayden, said that her nurse saw dogs licking up Robert Emmet's blood under the scaffold in Thomas Street, and women soaking it up with their handkerchiefs. I said I once talked with a man who had helped his father run a food-stall at O'Connell's meeting at Tara, bringing the provender up by canal boat from Kevin's Port to Kilmessan. Sigerson went furthest back. He said that a teacher of his—a Donegal man who had been a tutor to

83

the sons of Louis Philippe—saw Wolfe Tone smiling at the walls of Derry Gaol when he was taken there after his capture from the French ship in Lough Swilly.

It startles me now to think that my friend was born more than a hundred and thirty years ago and that I was part of this sort of talk for twenty years around his dinner table. The conversation remains in my mind as typical. It most often ran on Irish literature or history, but there was a French atmosphere about it that came from the doctor's earliest years. His walls were hung with fragments of tapestry, French paintings and pastels. His furniture was largely French, Louis XIV and XV, and when we rose after dinner from the high-backed, stamped leather chairs and from the striped tablecloth, it was my privilege to carry the branched candlesticks upstairs to the drawing room where there was still older French furniture and *objets d'art,* cabinets filled with French miniatures and portfolios stuffed with drawings, engravings and mezzotints. A Raffaello drawing, now in our National Gallery, came from one of those portfolios. He took pleasure in going through them. Not all were in mint condition. There was an old French friend of the doctor's there one evening about the time the Versailles Treaty was being dictated. He said he felt at home in this French interior, and in an undertone added slyly to me that like France it was calling out for reparations. The doctor was conservative of the things he liked. At home he preferred candles to electric light; branch candelabra lit both dining-room and drawing-room. There was no telephone and when he went abroad to his lectures or patients he drove out in an old cab. He looked and had the manners of an old French savant, his consulting room might have come out of Balzac. And there was nothing odd in this, because he went to Paris as a schoolboy in 1855, and again for post-graduate education, returning there year after year throughout his long life. He was sent to Paris just after Louis Napoleon's *coup d'état* and used to say that as a boy passing through two capitals he thought Dublin a much finer city than

London—the Thames embankment had not yet been built—and Paris was more like Dublin. He was already living in history. His lycée was in the Rue de l'Enfer in the heart of the Latin quarter in a house that once was Châteaubriand's and was earlier lived in by Louise de la Vallière. It was a spartan school where the boys in winter broke ice in their wash basins and their thin red wine was ironically styled 'Abondance' from its plenitude of water. His closest comrade was a Cavaignac, grandson of the *conventionnel* who had voted Louis XVI's execution and son of the general who, after the revolution of 1848, had mercilessly suppressed the 'red' rising against the new Assembly, and had then run second against Louis Napoleon for the presidency of the short-lived Republic. At school, young Sigerson got first place in a class of forty in Greek and Latin prose, botany and drawing, and second in history, German, and even in French literature. When prize-winning day came the Irish boy proudly went up to receive his prizes from the *aumonier* of the Emperor. Cavaignac, who sat beside him and had got other awards, stubbornly refused to answer to his name when it was called, or accept any gift from the hands of the usurper's deputy. The Irish schoolboy was beginning to understand the republican spirit.

In his post-graduate years at the Salpetrière his master was Charcot—leader of a new school in the treatment of nervous diseases—and another pupil was Sigmund Freud. Three-quarters of a century later, Sigerson was to attend Charcot's centenary celebration at the Sorbonne, as a representative of the National University of Ireland. Charcot's son, the Antarctic explorer, used to visit Clare Street not infrequently, a man sturdily built like his father and with his father's head, the head of Caesar and his father's eyes, the eyes of an eagle. There were also amongst Sigerson's friends and teachers in Paris, Claude Bernard the physiologist, Pasteur, and outside medicine Henri Martin the historian and Gambetta. Once, when on holiday in Paris,

Sigerson pointed out to me Claude Bernard's statue outside the École de Médicine. He said he often walked past that spot with Bernard and told him that his statue would one day be erected there. Similarly, looking at the monument to Gambetta which used to be at the Louvre, he said he crossed the *Place* with Gambetta when the Tuileries lay in ruins after the Commune. He asked Gambetta if they proposed to rebuild the palace. Gambetta was categorical in his reply; he would never consent to restore the relics of the Second Empire. Sigerson wondered whether he had not already ear-marked a desirable site for his own memorial.

On that holiday we used to meet regularly at the Cabinet des Estampes where he would collate and compare his last acquisitions of miniatures and engravings with the examples in that rich treasury. Then to dinner at Véfour's after an apéritif at the Café de la Régence. Between them lies the Palais Royal, which for all its historic associations from Mazarin to the gay days of the Directoire, was dull enough when I first knew the quarter. Shop windows fringing the neglected garden held cheap vulgarities and alternated incongruously with a display of the dry stalks of ministerial statistics and colonial vegetables. I saw the gardens revive with the introduction of Rodin's Victor Hugo, seated like a Neptune in gloomy meditation on rocks by a stagnant pool; then came a more exciting figure in bronze of another poet and revolutionary orator, Camille Desmoulins, leaping from a chair to pluck from overhead the green leaves of liberty, and to end the story, the present well-conceived restoration of the gardens to be promptly filled with joyous troops of children. Véfour's, now dizzy with modernity and starred by Michelin, has survived from the eighteenth century. When Sigerson brought me there it was much as Balzac described it, but somnolent as the cat that drowsed by Madame's desk, and quiet as the old gentlemen who sat playing their dominoes. The doctor would tell me of his youth when the narrow Rue Vivienne behind the garden was a principal thoroughfare and the Palais Royal was the hub of Paris. Véfour's remains memorable because there Sigerson introduced me to a dish of frogs, followed by *pieds de porc à la Ste Ménéhoule,* more simply recognized by us as pigs' *crubeens.* The doctor was not a gourmet, but he liked regional dishes like the *drisheens* of his Queen's College, Cork, days. He expected things to appear on his table in their right seasonal order; the young mountain mutton coming down from Wicklow in spring, the Michaelmas goose at her proper season, colcannon for All Souls' Day, and so forth. No. 3 Clare Street was the last private house in which I partook of sloke served from its special eighteenth-century silver sauce boat. Does it now survive anywhere, even at the King's Inns?

Ireland and France made a very agreeable mélange, and what the doctor learned from France in the way of science and the arts he strove to repay. He would ill brook any slighting of that country, but came to its defence only less warmly than to his own. At his table, and indeed on every occasion, he showed a magnanimity and a generosity of mind that forbade mean speech or the belittlement of others. He gave glad recognition to the slightest work of Irish value. If at his table a word of even deserved criticism was spoken of anyone who had served Ireland, there inevitably came from that well-stored mind the counter-balancing recital of service.

Where Sigerson was not Irish or French he was Norse. His name bears witness, and though he was born in 1836 at Holyhill near Strabane in County Tyrone where his family had long lived, the Sigerson Castle at Ballinskelligs, County Kerry, was its original habitat. At any rate, when the name of a new acquaintance gave him the chance to impute a Norse ancestry to him, he was quickly enrolled on their side. That was my early fate. He affiliated me to Olaf Cuaran, the Norse king of Dublin, and I was rallied to his support when at table, as was common, new wars of the Gael and the Gall broke out. Irish though he might be, he held Brian Boroimhe suspect. There was one evening when the manner of the great king's death was thrown against the doctor. He counter-attacked in defence of the Norse slayer, and his description of the unchivalrous execution done upon Bruadair tore our hearts as the Munsterman tore Bruadair's entrails. It was then I found myself proclaiming Sigerson's victory in a quatrain, a parody I must claim as my own:

> In vain they rebuke and revile us,
> Still stand we, our hands to the hilt,
> On our side are Vikings and virtue,
> On theirs, the Gael and the guilt.

If I recall all these trivialities and shy away from Sigerson's real achievement, it is because I am not competent to appraise its variety and quality. Much of his scientific work is now outdated like Charcot's, which he translated. That is the fate of most scientists whose papers and opuscula are like coral reefs built of their own dead shells. But a man is known by his friends and fellows. Tyndall praised Sigerson's work. Darwin proposed him as Fellow of the Linnaean Society. Claude Bernard, Pasteur and Charcot were, as I have said, his friends, and to the French historian Henry Martin, I can add the great names of Mommsen and Acton. He grew intimate with Acton in the late 'sixties when Acton was associated with *The Chronicle, The North British* and *The Home and Foreign Review*. It was then, at Acton's request, that he began the studies which he expanded and published in 1871 as the *History of Irish Land Tenures*. Lecky found them of great historical value, and read in proof to Gladstone they influenced his first Irish Land Act. When Acton and his fellow-editors sought the services of Mommsen as foreign correspondent, Mommsen consented only when he was satisfied through Sigerson that they would be colleagues in an enterprise sympathetic to both.

He was a young man, a student in Queen's College, Cork, when in 1860 he published his *Poets and Poetry of Munster* in continuation of James Clarence Mangan's work. Presently he took his M.D. and continued his studies abroad, but the quiet ways of literature and science did not contain his passion for Ireland. He found one outlet in journalism and lifted it to literature, and another in comradeship with men quite unlikely to advance his professional career. The Fenians, Kickham and John O'Leary were his intimates, and when he had finished his postgraduate study he quietly, though not himself a Fenian, placed himself by their side. It is not easy in our day to realize how much courage and tenacity it meant in 1862 to take the stand Sigerson then took and unswervingly held. He came to Dublin, to a university chair and to private practice, with something of a continental reputation won from his association with the masters of the new learning of the Nancy school and the Salpetrière. He had unique gifts of personality and his training was admirably fitted to display them. He did not choose to exploit these talents for professional advancement in the manner of the fashionable physician, exceeding all bounds in 'keeping others waiting', like the women distinguished in *The Instructions of King Cormac Mac Art*. However, in his case 'the others' were the rich whose carriages were kept waiting while he attended to his poor. This was dangerous. But to taint a professional career with tincture of letters was more dangerous, and with the virus of Irish letters, stark insanity. To add political writing to that—and by politics one always meant, naturally, non-viceregal politics—was criminal madness. He consorted with, defended, healed Fenians when Fenians were the object of opprobrium, though he himself, no more than his *anam-chara* John O'Leary, was never, as I have said, a sworn member of the Brotherhood. When *The Irish People* was suppressed he edited *The Irishman* which replaced it, and his article, 'The Holocaust', written in November 1867 on the Manchester Martyrs, stirred men's souls then as did Dr

O'Dwyer's letters to General Maxwell in 1916. As editor of *The Irishman,* he had John Mitchel as his Paris correspondent. Curiously enough, Pigott, whose forgery was unmasked in the Parnell-*Times* libel case, was then its owner, taking no part, however, in the editorial side. We have the forger's opinion of him in one of Pigott's letters which delated Irish nationalists to Chief Secretary Foster: 'Dr Sigerson, a man who, to my own knowledge, has written more treason, treason-felony, sedition and incitements to murder and outrage than any other living man in Ireland at least.'[1]

As Professor of the Catholic University he wrote and spoke over a great space of years in the struggle for equality in university education, but other traces of his advocacy are not so easily tracked down, so liberal was he with his pen. I have heard it said that he wrote the peroration of the speech of one counsel for the traversers at the State Trial of Parnell in 1881, and that he supplied material for Parnell's address to Congress when, in the succession of Lafayette and Kossuth, Parnell spoke in the American House. It should be possible to detect his share in that address even if shorn of his characteristic vocabulary.

His historical studies were continued in *Two Centuries of Irish History* edited by Bryce in 1888 and enlarged in his *Last Independent Parliament of Ireland.* In 1896 Acton was entrusted with the editing of the *Cambridge Modern History* and sought his collaboration. The periods of Canning and Grey had been, he said, allotted to Lecky and Walpole; he was 'hoping very fervently indeed that you will occupy another section with Irish history from Sarsfield to O'Connell.'[2]

His studies in Irish and Irish poetry, which began in 1860 in Queen's College, Cork, under W. M. Hennessy who edited the *Annals of Ulster,* bore their full fruit more than thirty years later

1. Letter 29 August, 1883, *Report of Prisons Commission.* Vol. 5, p. 592; see also T. D. Sullivan: *Recollections of Troubled Times in Irish Politics,* Dublin 1905.
2. Acton to Sigerson, 2 December 1896.

in *The Bards of the Gael and the Gall*. This anthology is, I suppose, his most characteristic work. Directed to the general public, it supplied a scholarly and most persuasive conspectus of our poetry from the earliest period to the end of the eighteenth century. Much of its challenging material has been checked and supplemented by later specialists, but in the 'nineties it stood alone, and for combined range and discriminating choice of fine poetry this Pisgah prospect of our poetic literature has hardly been bettered. A letter from Imogen Guiney, who published a fine edition of Mangan, mentions it as 'an eye-opener'. With Hyde's *Love Songs of Connaught* it was in the hands of all our young writers, and it had a profound effect on the revival of Irish letters.

Sigerson exerted the same influence in a more general way through the National Literary Society. He was in the chair at its founding meeting at the Rotunda in 1892; the other speakers were W. B. Yeats, Maud Gonne, Father Tom Finlay and John O'Leary, and he delivered its inaugural lecture at the Antient Concert Rooms two months later. Under his presidency the Society was foster-parent of the new revival which included the Feis Ceoil as well as the theatre, and his own long series of inaugural lectures left few aspects of Irish life untouched.

His manner and bearing gave further distinction to these addresses. More justly than Lavery's *soigné* portrait in the Dublin Municipal Gallery, his own *Saga of King Lir* depicts him:

> Magnificent he stood; his red-brown locks
> From ample brow and kingly head flowed down,
> A lambent flame . . .

In *Finnegans Wake*, where in various forms his Norse name frequently bobs up, we have another artist's vision of him. Here Joyce's anti-self finds himself leaning against an ambiguous figure; in part, an ancient pillar-stone awakening ancestral memories; in part a Norseman, 'the butter-blond Sigurdson'. Small wonder then, that when Augustine Birrell, the Irish Chief Secretary, paid his first visit to University College on the eve of his University Bill, he saw this Viking apparition approach with amazement. He enquired who he was. 'Such a monument', he said, 'must surely have a university to hold it.'

Sigerson's speech, for all its lurking humour, had the massive dignity of his build and bearing. Andrew Marvell wrote of Milton's Latin eloquence: 'When I consider', he said, 'how equally it turns and rises with so many figures, it seems to me a Trajan's column in whose winding ascent we see embossed the several monuments of his learned victories.' So did the doctor's address seem to me, or like a Roman aqueduct, lifted above the plain, bringing clear water from old fountain-heads. At the National Literary Society his audience relished the wit and point of those brief addresses which closed the proceedings. We waited eagerly for the glancing irony that shot through the folds of his ceremonious speech. His art allied the formality of the French *éloge* to Irish wit. Not to him belonged the 'untameable squadrons of irrelevant eloquence'. His deliberate phrases advanced like the classic phalanx bristling with bright spears, and the shafts of his wit lost nothing from the contrast of uplifted eyebrow and humorous twinkling eyes with the slow, sonorous voice and the courteous gravity with which he bore himself.

I give one example of his speech. Just as the National Literary Society had given its platform to Douglas Hyde, in the months before Hyde and John MacNeill with Father O'Growney founded the Gaelic League, so also the Society befriended the Irish Literary Theatre. Yeats's *The Countess Cathleen* was about to have its first performance. A newspaper controversy had been stirred up about the play by Frank Hugh O'Donnell, a virulent opponent in London of W. B. Yeats. Sigerson had no sympathy with O'Donnell's violent criticism of the play, contained in a brochure published in London some days before its production.

This is how he dealt with it. Having referred to obstacles surmounted by other Irish pioneer groups, he proceeded:

> These have triumphed not without difficulties. When the
> Celtic soldiers of Brennus climbed the Tarpeian Rock the
> alarm was given to the Capitol by the ever-vigilant geese.
> Since that time there has been enmity between the geese
> and the Gael. Whenever the Celts raise their heads the hiss
> of the geese arises also. . . . There are some writers who take
> their quills from the wings of the Capitoline geese, some
> also from the active though fretful porcupine. . . . But that
> is availing no longer. We should rather dread the one great
> defect of the Celts, their hyper-critical faculty: *Gallicus
> Gallico Lupus* said the old observer.

Before my time Yeats was a visitor to Clare Street when
Sigerson's daughters, Dora and Hester, along with Catherine
Tynan, were reading and writing verse together. The quartet
also crystal-gazed. There was an afternoon, Dora told me, when
they were so seated around the crystal near a window and Yeats
was asked what he saw: 'I see a man winding and waving his
arms to and fro; I see a man with coloured scarves waving and
winding his arms to and fro, to and fro.' Passing by chance
through the room, the doctor paused to observe what was going
on, and for answer pointed across the street to Price's Medical
Hall where, at a window glowing with the great gilt and lac-
quered globes of coloured water that marked the apothecary, a
window cleaner was at work.

When the Irish Literary Societies were launched in London and
Dublin and Yeats differed from Gavan Duffy on the choice of
proposed publications, it was Yeats who invited Sigerson and
John O'Leary to arbitrate their differences, and we have seen
how Sigerson championed the cause of the Irish Literary Theatre
in which Yeats was the prime mover. As the years passed, their

ways fell apart.Why? Yeats, it is true, had no sympathy with the scientific intelligence, but no one could accuse Sigerson, as Yeats accused Wells, of having a mind like a sewing machine. Perhaps Sigerson was too much of an extrovert, as the window-cleaning episode shows, and had no interest in magic. Anyway I never met Yeats at Sigerson's house.

At his own table or in public I have never heard Sigerson fail to recognize Yeats's genius, though a quizzical uplifting of eyebrows might query at times its magical or mythological content. Yeats's later acerbity, I am pretty sure, originated in the controversy that gathered about the first performance of Synge's *Playboy,* when Sigerson read a paper to the National Literary Society on 'The Irish Peasant'. The paper, which was freely open to discussion, was much too dispassionate and far-ranging to please so passionate an advocate and friend of Synge as was Yeats.

I spent many an evening with him in a lonely house in his later years, when the two of us would once a week make our slow way through his miniatures and dirty, ragged portfolios, breaking off for a short spell at midnight to share a bottle of wine and sandwiches, before resuming the task I had suggested of cataloguing his collection. I learned a great deal from those drawings and prints, however imperfect their condition. Each item was the starting point for a new excursion into French history, or an excuse for reminiscence about Paris antiquaries, scientists or politicians, or Irish figures who had passed into history. He never lost touch with contemporary events, but such ripples as the Abbey row were to him one of the commonplaces of life, and not confined to the *gens irritabile*. In his long life—for he was nearly ninety when he died—he had seen and shared in greater vicissitudes, viewing them, some ironically, and some with anxious solicitude. In his last years one touched him deeply. It was when in civil strife, fanatical 'irregulars' sent him a message that they would burn his house as they had burned the houses of other Irishmen, Colonel Moore and Sir Horace Plunkett, if

he remained, as he was, a member of the Irish Senate. I am glad
to think, however, that it was men of my generation and way
of thinking, who honoured themselves by calling him to the
Oireachtas to preside over the first meeting of an Irish Senate,
for none of us who knew him will greatly quarrel with the
historian Acton who wrote of him as 'the best Irishman I have
known'.

6 University College and the Countess Cathleen

HAD I been in University College a few months earlier in 1899, I would have assisted at an affair which was still the subject of discussion in the Michaelmas term. Its rumours have not since wholly died down; but in the interval the truth of the matter has been so twisted that I think it well to set down the facts, checked by contemporary proof, as they remain in my memory. The affair was neither the first nor the last of these lively manifestations of popular feeling which are long associated with the theatre in Dublin and which are everywhere and at all times a sign and proof of the theatre's vitality. It concerned the inauguration of the Irish Literary Theatre and the first perform- ance of Yeats's *The Countess Cathleen* in the Antient Concert Rooms on 8 May 1899. The play occasioned a students' demon- stration, and it was followed by a statement from them, published in the Dublin press two days later.

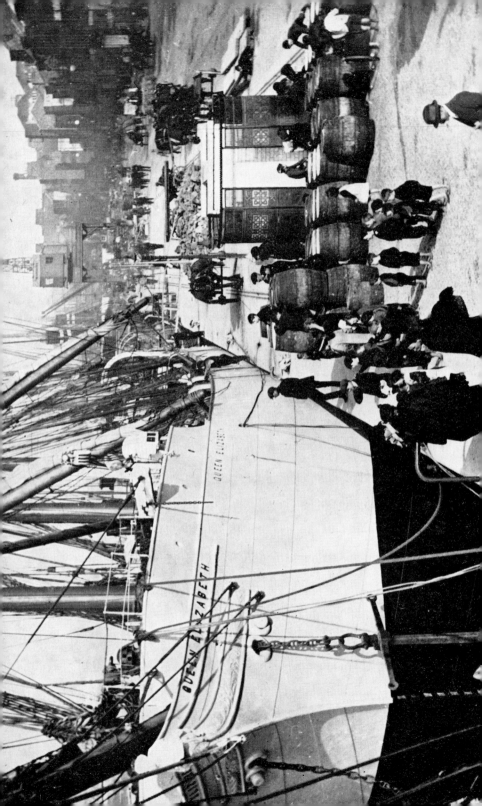

Years before the dramatic movement had taken its first direction under the guidance of W. B. Yeats, Edward Martyn and George Moore, the play had been published in London in a volume entitled *The Countess Cathleen and Various Legends and Lyrics* with a quotation from Paracelsus on its title page. In a lecture to the National Literary Society in 1899 Yeats said that he had not intended to include work of his own in the opening repertoire of the new theatre. Here, however, was a play which had passed the Horation period of seclusion. In its remote and romantic setting it presented with sufficient stagecraft a sufficiently dramatic fable lit up by many lines and images of fine poetry. To that extent it was well chosen by the directors as the first step in the restoration of the theatre to art. The founders, however, and its very name, held out the promise of something more than a Bedford Park or garden suburb venture. Its prospectus set out the desire of the promoters 'to bring down upon the stage the deepest thoughts and emotions of Ireland' and it was heralded as 'a vehicle for the literary expression of the national thoughts and ideals of Ireland such as has not hitherto been in existence'. Already in the preface to the 1892 edition of his play Yeats had written of it as 'an attempt to mingle personal thought and feeling with the beliefs and customs of Christian Ireland', and furthermore, in his application to the municipal authorities for the usual temporary licence to perform, Edward Martyn, on behalf of his associates, represented Yeats's play, as well as his own *Heather Field* as 'exemplifications of Irish life'.[1] On this score the play was open to debate. As the first step in the establishment of an Irish theatre, it did not seem to live up, so to speak, to the Articles of Association. Its action turned on the self-sacrifice of a noble lady moving amongst a Catholic peasantry terrified by famine and crazed by superstition. They are selling their souls to demon-merchants. Famine and proselytism were well-known associated

1. Denis Gwynn, *Edward Martyn and the Irish Revival*, London 1930, 126.

G

phenomena in Ireland far into the nineteenth century and within everyone's memory. Yeats's theme and his treatment of it aroused misgivings amongst the promoters, and indeed in himself, months before the production. Some weeks before the actual perform- ance, controversy became public. It started in London with Frank Hugh O'Donnell, as Yeats asserted, and it was envenomed with what had every appearance of a personal vendetta. O'Donnell, a one-time member of parliament, loved polemics and sharpened his fretful quills against every man. He was in turn Parnellite and anti-Parnellite, episcopophagous, anti-clerical and anti-Jesuit. Arthur Griffith described him in this affray as one who 'tomahawked with the savage delight of a Chocktaw'. He called Yeats a 'meandering decadent with a diseased mind'.

But the original text had been in the hands of the public for seven years and had been read by some University College students. *Inter alia* it set forth the fall of a little shrine of the Blessed Virgin in Séamus Rua's cabin upon the advent of the demon-merchants, and the stage direction describes him 'kicking it to pieces'. In later editions of the play, Yeats changed this scene and deleted these incidents. At the same time, quite un- fairly, he retained in his notes to successive editions his misrepre- sentation of the students' protest which was largely based on the passages deleted. Furthermore, Yeats was later to say that the action of the play was in no country in particular, but lay in a region of myth and symbol. The original printed text, however, lays the scene 'in Ireland in old times' and Lionel Johnson who wrote the prologue wrote also in the advance issue of the official organ of the theatre, *Beltaine,* that the action takes place at the end of the Irish sixteenth century.

These dubious themes, the stage kicking of Our Lady's shrine the sale of their souls by our peasants, and an affair of stuffing, away the soul of a priest and a pig in a bag, were developed in full diapason by Frank Hugh O'Donnell.[2] They were taken up before the performance by the Healyite *Daily Nation* in hardly less bitter leading articles and correspondence, and were more temperately debated by the *Freeman's Journal* and in the National Literary Society. It was in this atmosphere of expectation and controversy that a group of University College students attended the first performance. At that production some of the objectionable passages were, as from later editions of the text, omitted, and the shrine was not kicked about the stage. But the students found plenty of matter for both hissing and applause, though the manifestation of their double opinion was less of an interruption than was the presence of the police whom the management had thoughtfully provided.

The play was, on the whole, received by the press in a reasonably friendly fashion. The *Daily Nation* remained, of course, violently recalcitrant, although Tim Healy, like John Dillon and John Redmond, was a guarantor of the new enterprise. Its kicks were the more vigorous, being directed quite as much at the *Freeman's Journal* as at Yeats. The *Freeman* had lent steady support to the proposed theatre. Its editor, W. H. Brayden, himself a former student of University College, was a man of generous culture whose kindly welcome to a young student I have reason to remember as he sat in his dusty little editorial office in Prince's Street, a large, benevolent figure, with a perpetual air of weary omniscience.

T. P. Gill, then editor of the *Daily Express,* and T. W. Rolleston were recognized mouthpieces for the new theatre. Another supporter was Jack McGrath, the friend of Lionel Johnson who dedicated to him his poem *Inisfail.* He adopted as his own the defence put forward by Yeats that the play had as little to do with any place or time as an *auto* by Calderon; that

2. Frank Hugh O'Donnell's diatribes were later issued by him in brochures entitled *Faith for Gold* and *Blasphemy and Degradation.* He finally elaborated them into his *Stage Irishman of the Pseudo-Celtic Drama,* London 1904.

the peasants should be looked for, not in history, but in one's own heart, and that the poet's imagination was working wholly in the region of myth and symbol. The *Irish Times* looked down its viceregal nose at a manifestation that was something in the nature of a party squabble, but at the same time thought that the changes made in the text 'were wisely arranged, for certainly the play offends, and most unnecessarily, very great susceptibilities in the ordinary play-going Irish man and woman. . . . The very idea as assiduously advertised of the Irish Literary Theatre is to reflect Ireland, its manners, its customs, its ideas, its thoughts, aye, even its superstitions, if you will'.

The *United Irishman* was obviously embarrassed by Arthur Griffith's friendship with Maud Gonne to whom the play was inscribed, and by Yeats's share, however slight, in the recent '98 celebrations. Determined, as usual, to judge everything in the light of its value in the fight for Irish freedom, Griffith is plainly ill at ease in his criticism. He deplores Frank Hugh O'Donnell's Red Indian technique as little as he approves of the *Independent's* description of the play as a *magnum opus*. He prefers Mr Yeats's earlier and simple verse; he believes that plays requiring much thought are unlikely to catch the popular mind in Ireland; he finds the stage atmosphere of the Antient Concert Rooms un-natural and un-Irish; he recognizes there, not Ireland but Gothic grotesques and Teutonic dolls. But he equally deplores the misguided, unthinking action of the students who set up the cry of Thomas Davis against Yeats. Further familiarity with Davis would bring them to other conclusions; Mr Yeats is a patriot, however, etc., etc.

Such debates never end, but the action of the students them-selves closed with a letter of protest which was signed by some thirty of their number. There were about one hundred and fifty students in the arts faculty of the college at that time. In later editions of his play Yeats said the letter was written on the per-suasion of a politician and a newspaper (i.e. F. H. O'Donnell and

The Nation)—this statement is without foundation. Equally
untrue and wholly preposterous is a later statement made by
Stanislaus Joyce that 'the budding mob-leaders among the
students (were) egged on by a political intriguer, Father Finlay,
S.J.'[3]

The students' protest was the direct answer to, and followed
immediately upon, a provocative sentence in the *Freeman's
Journal* notice which ridiculed the conduct of a 'knot of less than
a dozen disorderly boys who evidently mistook the whole moral
significance of the play'.[4] The signatories based their protest on
a contrast of the play with Yeats's undertaking 'to put on the
stage plays dealing with Irish subjects or reflecting Irish ideas and
sentiments'. Its author, they said, 'represents the Irish peasant as a
crooning barbarian, crazed with morbid superstition who having
added the Catholic faith to his store of superstition sells that
faith for gold or bread in the proving of famine'. They find the
play 'not Irish in subject and its characters travesties of the Irish
Catholic Celt. This view of the national character is not justified
by the history of our famines.' The letter was signed amongst
others by Tom Kettle, Frank Skeffington, and George Clancy.
Other signatories included a future President of University
College, Cork, the first Chief Justice of the Irish Free State and
one of his colleagues on the Supreme Court. Absent were a few
names of men active in College societies. Professor Felix Hackett
has pointed out that missing names included six out of the ten
speakers to Arthur Clery's address on *The Theatre* delivered to
the College Literary and Historical Society only two months
before.[5] Clery's own name, for example, does not appear, nor
William Dawson's, though both were auditors of the Society and

3. Stanislaus Joyce, *My Brother's Keeper*, London 1958, 94.
4. The letter appeared in the *Freeman's Journal* 10 May 1899. The article
which provoked the letter was in the issue of the preceding day.
5. See James Meenan (ed.), *Centenary History of the Literary and Historical
Society University College, Dublin 1855–1955*.

both were keenly interested in everything to do with the theatre. Their absence proves nothing except the worthlessness of a statement like Herbert Gorman's 'that all the students were gently coerced into signing it. That is, all except one. Joyce, contemptuously, refused to add his signature to the rest.'[6]

Whoever wants the opinion of a qualified and impartial observer will find it in a letter from T. W. Rolleston which appeared in the same issue of the *Freeman's Journal* (10 May) as the students' protest. Rolleston, a member of the Rhymers' Club, a friend of Yeats and of John O'Leary, dealt with the incident in considered terms:

> As it happens I was sitting close to the 'dozen disorderly boys' referred to by your correspondent in his account of the performance on Monday night. It appeared to me that their expressions of disapproval were not exactly disorderly. There is unquestionably much in the play that must put a strain on the patriotic and religious feelings of an audience not accustomed to look at dramatic literature from a purely artistic standpoint, and, paradoxical as it may seem, it is only very unlettered or very highly cultivated audiences that are capable of doing that. An audience or any members of it have a right to express disapproval as well as to applaud. It would be the death of drama to abrogate this right as Goethe sought to do at Weimar with the natural result that the audience at Weimar swept *Iphegenie* and *Egmont* from the stage and went wild over the performance of an accomplished poodle. The young men, there were about twenty of them, who hissed and hooted at certain passages last night appeared to me to be probably Royal University students. They expressed their sentiments with vigour but in a perfectly gentlemanlike manner. They flung no insults at the

6. H. Gorman, *James Joyce*, London 1941, 60.

author or the company; they made no attempt seriously to interfere with the performance and they applauded as vigorously as anyone, nay, they even led the applause at some of the fine and touching passages in the play. Undoubtedly, the ferocious attacks and incitements to violence made from certain quarters during the last few days had much to do with the warm demonstrations of sympathy made by the audience. But they did not inspire the opposition in the theatre. The impression left in my mind by the whole affair was that a representative Dublin audience had splendidly vindicated in the teeth of bitter prejudice and hostility an author's right to a fair hearing of his work and also that the hostile element in the audience had expressed itself in a manner which, if one is permitted to be hostile at all, had no trace of malice or stupid violence.

Yeats, as I have said, charged the students in this affair with concerted, hostile action at the persuasion of a politician and a newspaper. Parrot-voices repeated this charge and added more explicitly the charge of sectarian obtuseness. Anyone who knew the temper and opinions of the College at that date would more easily imagine that any opinion of Frank Hugh O'Donnell or *The Nation* on any topic would sway them—if such students were in any respect tractable—in a contrary direction. No one ever accused Yeats of being ingenuous. He was always an astute and wily controversialist. Years later he made radical changes from his original text as well as from its already revised acting version. The first two scenes—he notes in later editions—'are almost wholly new and throughout the play I have added or left out such passages as a stage experience of some years showed me encumbered the action.' These were the very scenes and encumbrances to which the students had taken exception but in 1899 Yeats preferred to represent the issue as solely touching the liberty of the artist and—with certain deviations on his part into

Pauline theology—a proper critical approach. It is fair to say that the audience of 1899 was concerned with it solely as the first play to be selected for the repertory of a theatre which proclaimed itself Irish and literary. With one voice it applauded its fine lines. The student audience dared to anticipate the author in rejecting the magical flummery that obscured rather than enriched the poet's intention. Relying on the text and the declared aims of the theatre, it repudiated the fable and much of the action as a safe foundation for an Irish theatre. The ambivalence of shrines and quicken boughs may be matter for Frazerian debate; but stage directions for statue-kicking, even though not carried out, do not, to a reader of the text with regard for its circumstances, appear admissible even on the purely dramatic plane. It is as likely to be repugnant as the roasting of the Playboy at a turf fire. Similar questions were settled in Athens many years ago, and the deletions, restorations, revisions and emendations which the protean Yeats wrought in his texts are evidence certainly of his artistry but also of his insecurity.

Rolleston's balanced judgement was confirmed more incisively by Stephen Gwynn who gave invaluable aid to the theatre movement and, more ambiguously, by Max Beerbohm who speaking at the Shelbourne dinner two days later confessed that, being a stranger to Dublin, he did not know if the students were right or wrong but that if he had the honour of being Irish-born he would be very angry.

The letter of protest now reads to me as a composite and hurried performance with Tom Kettle as the most evidently single influence. Certain sentences and phrases bear his unmistakable stamp—I can hear his voice leaning in characteristic fashion on the vowel sounds of the 'crooning barbarian'. The introduction of the Elizabethan, Carew, obviously derives from Lionel Johnson's dating of the play to the end of the sixteenth century but why the play should be described as of German origin eludes me; Arthur Griffith, as we have seen, also found in it Teutonic dolls. This search for origins can lead us inconclusively far. Yeats used the same theme in his *Irish Fairy and Folk Tales* in 1892. The story he prints there is called 'The Countess Kathleen O'Shea'; the occurrence of the surname had always struck me as curious at a moment when attention was elsewhere so tragically directed to this ill-omened name. Yeats's brief footnote to the story runs: 'This was quoted in a London Irish newspaper. I am unable to find out the original source.' In the 1904 edition of his poems (Fisher Unwin) he makes a fuller disclosure. He says he found the story in an Irish paper and heard afterwards that it had been translated from *Les Matinées de Timothy Trimm* many years earlier and had been drifting about the Irish press ever since. The heroine's improbable name was Comtesse Ketty O'Donnor and a certain Leo Lespes was the compiler. Yeats prints the French text *in extenso* with some lines translated from a ballad said by Lespes to have been sung in the streets of Dublin and Cork. Yeats further mentions, as a variant, the story taken down by William Larminie from a story-teller in Glencolumkille, County Donegal, but this tale of 'The Woman who went to Hell' has little, if any, connection with the poet's dramatic fable. Another fragmentary gleam of light is thrown on the source by Fr George O'Neill, S.J., a member of the National Literary Society. In an article published in *The New Ireland Review* he treats the whole subject with his habitual courtesy and candour and on the point of origin has this to add: 'It is a fact less insisted on but now admitted that the subject of the *Countess Kathleen* has no root either in Irish history or in Irish legend. It came amongst us a complete stranger, picked up by Mr John Augustus O'Shea in his rambles among French popular traditions and remains a *wunder-kind* whom no one cares to welcome.'[7]

7. O'Neill, 'The Inauguration of the Irish Literary Theatre', *The New Ireland Review* Vol. X, 1899. Writing to Lady Gregory in 1900, Yeats says he has found another Franco-Irish source in the British Museum: see Alan Wade, *Letters of W. B. Yeats*, London 1954, 316.

With this interpolation of a third O'Shea into the narrative
I may pass from this confused controversy. Whether the students
were right or wrong is now of little moment. They assisted in
making the next night's performance of Martyn's *Heather Field*
a success which nearly approached a triumph and they remained
for the rest of their days appreciative supporters of the theatre.
In the company of some one or other of them for many years
I missed no other first performance of the Irish Literary Theatre
or its successors and experience has not changed my opinion that
the spontaneous, friendly or hostile reaction of the audience,
immediately and audibly expressed, spells life to the theatre.

Birrell, the Chief Secretary, said something relevant to such
reactions when he gave evidence about the Abbey Theatre in
1916 to the Royal Commission on the Rebellion in Ireland. 'I was
often', he said, 'amazed at the literary detachment and courage
of the playwright, the relentlessness of the actors and actresses
and the patience and comprehension of the audience.' This first
imbroglio has remained of some significance in the history of our
theatre and has led me to dwell on it at length. Its echoes sounded
through many subsequent debates in the College. It contained
the seeds of later development in the theatre and revealed diver-
gent aims in the promoters. A college student, sitting apart from
the others on the balcony, was presently to discuss these aims
and divergencies in a pamphlet named characteristically *The
Day of the Rabblement*.

In the spring of 1907 a whirlpool of debate engulfed every
society, club, bar or drawing-room, when every good Dublin
citizen paraded his peasant origin and his intimate knowledge of
country life. I was present at the much misrepresented first performance of *The Playboy of the Western World* and find the
reaction of the audience still grossly distorted. So late as 28
January 1963 I find a special correspondent of *The Times* reporting
an interview with one of the surviving actors, Mr J. M. Kerrigan,
and putting into his mouth the statement that he 'remembers

Synge on the stage as the bottles and garbage flew, during the first performance of *The Playboy*.'

My friend, Mr Kerrigan, wrote to me later repudiating this statement. He said that 'no missiles were thrown on the stage during the run of *The Playboy* at the Abbey'; that 'Synge never appeared on the stage during the performance of the opening night, and the old Abbey audience were not in the habit of bringing empty bottles to the theatre', and finally he authorized me to say 'I emphatically deny any such statement was made or even suggested'.

My own recollection of that night is clear. Abbey audiences had been won over to Synge by his *Riders to the Sea* three years earlier. It was again most warmly received when presented on the night in question before *The Playboy*. The first act of *The Playboy* was received in wholly friendly fashion and with much applause. It so happened that I met Synge with other friends during the first interval and congratulated him duly on his evident success. This success was so evident that he said in reply that he regretted having made a few verbal cuts during rehearsal in deference to his actors. During the second act the friendly atmosphere chilled and the curtain went down on a receptive but undemonstrative audience. In the third act sporadic hissing was heard and from the entrance of Christy Mahon's father it became more general. When at its close the neighbours hitch the rope around Christy to roast him at the fire and Pegeen blows the turf, preparing a lighted sod to scorch his shins, verbal protests came from all parts of the house. The play came to its final passages, not in disorder, for every word was heard, but in plain hostility. These episodes were played with unswerving realism. Admiration for a parricide had sunk in and cooled the audience, and later debate swirled around this *motif* as part of the manners and customs of Mayo. But I was and am satisfied that it was the unrelenting realism of the production in its last scene, a realism never again attempted in any of the later performances I have seen, that threw the audience into final revolt. Myself, I found it more revolting than even Shakespeare's gouging out of Gloucester's eyes in *King Lear*. There were, no doubt, the other factors of parricide, Pegeen's earlier behaviour, and some heightened language. We were living, it should be remembered, in 1907, unconditioned to excess in speech or action. Even so, bottles and garbage in my experience were not our form of dramatic criticism.

My friend, Mr Padraic Colum, who was present that Saturday evening with George Moore, corroborates what I have written and I still make bold to confirm an octogenarian's memory by reference to what two other friends and eyewitnesses have written. In a letter to John Quinn, AE (George W. Russell) describes the row at the Abbey during the next week as

> . . . really a newspaper row which got its ferocity to a great extent from certain defences made by unpopular people like 'Pat' (P. J. Kenny) the journalist, who would have it that *The Playboy* was a most accurate representation of Irish life. On the first night of the performance at which I was present there was a great deal of applause and only just at the last a little hissing or booing over one or two of the phrases and I am convinced that it would never have been much worse than that only for the defenders, who almost went to the point of stating that any Irish family would welcome a parricide. But, Synge, personally, was never unpopular. . . . *Riders to the Sea* performed every evening before *The Playboy* was received with tumultuous applause. *The Playboy* is a miraculous piece of writing, but I think, owing to the subject, it required to be acted with a great deal of phantasy. . . . The audience felt that they were really making a jest of parricide and father-beating. If in this first performance the father of the Playboy had been acted

more fantastically and less realistically, I am convinced that there would have been no row of any kind.[8]

This opinion of AE corresponds closely to my own.

The so-called Abbey row started the next week when hostile feeling had crystallized. The riotous demonstrations persisting during the week were of that social-political nature which lights up the history of the stage and is proof of a living theatre wherever it fortunately exists. Let me further introduce the testimony of Lady Gregory as reported by Wilfrid Scawen Blunt.[9] She wrote to him two months after these happenings: 'The first night', she said, 'passed fairly well with only a few hisses but on the second night there was an organized opposition and fearing mischief she sent for the police and afterwards there was a tumult every night of the week till the last performance when the opponents of the play got tired of their noise.' To my mind it was this ill-advised and unprecedented introduction of police that inflamed and prolonged the disturbances. No Dublin audience would brook such interference by police or lightly see demonstrators thrown out. In one notable case a perfectly innocent and well-known spectator was arrested and brought to court. All Dublin trooped to the Abbey to share in this new form of drama. A few members of the Arts Club and some T.C.D. students were enlisted to replace the police when their presence was too obviously obnoxious and absurd. The pit sang national songs. The enlisted claque took over the theatre piano and played *God save the King*. Everyone enjoyed themselves and I still have in memory of those nights some drawings by Orpen purporting, *inter alia*, to show Sir Hugh Lane, that gentle and elegant figure, in evening dress uplifting in the air, to throw him out, a disturber of the peace. The affair died down more reputably in two free-for-all debates. The first, *faute de mieux*, was presided

8. Alan Denson (ed.), *Letters from A.E.*. London 1961, 66-7.
9. W. S. Blunt, *My Diaries*, Vol. II, London 1919, 172.

over in the Abbey by 'Pat' who was cutting a journalistic dash in those days. The honours were carried away by John Butler Yeats, father of the poet and the painter, himself a painter whose merit is only now beginning to be recognized. Nonchalantly the old man strolled on to the platform, sketch-book as usual in his hands, and he was affectionately received. Discoursing more or less at random he alluded casually to the 'Island of Saints'. The catch phrase was applauded by some but when the old man with equal guile parenthetically continued, 'plaster saints', he brought the house down. From the second discussion, which was on Sigerson's paper at the National Literary Society, another phrase floats into my memory down the years. One of the speakers to the paper was the red-bearded Ulsterman, W. J. Lawrence, the well-known authority on the Elizabethan stage and on Irish dramatic history. Having in mind the posse of police who had been pouncing on comparatively or wholly innocent theatre-goers, he referred to the 'organized interruption of a cough'. It was not the first time that Lawrence had crossed Yeats's track. Addressing an audience in London, W. B. Yeats was describing some unusual Irish personalities and amongst them a red-headed Ulsterman, who at any meeting would rarely take anything but violent pedantic exception to the remarks of the previous speaker. 'If I were speaking in Dublin', he said, 'this man would be there.' A tall red beard rose from the back of the hall. In unmistakable Ulster Doric, he said, 'I am here.'

7   *Fellow Students and the Cui Bono*

Skeffington

A T the opening of the Michaelmas term of 1899 my name was entered on the roll of University College. The formality took place in the Bursar's room, a sober eighteenth-century apartment dignified with great stucco panels of Apollo and the Muses. When the new undergraduate had shaken hands with the Bursar and received his good wishes he shyly passed from his presence up the staircase of No. 85 to the Old Physics Theatre. He had no acquaintance amongst the students but this dereliction did not long endure. He was intercepted at the first landing by a senior student of quite unusual appearance, bearded, knicker-bockered and softcollared, of quick-firing speech and business-like address but none the less adroitly courteous. Frank Skeffington enormously flattered the newcomer by knowing his name and mentioning the distinction of a gold medal he had just won in the Senior Grade Intermediate examinations. He swiftly followed up his advantage by pointing out the plain duty which lay on me to join the Literary and Historical Society of which he was an officer. Obediently I entered my name on this roll and in that Society, as a dumb observer, I watched the development of many of my later friends. In that far from stagnant tank Frank Skeffington was the cat-fish. Already the restless propagandist that he ever was, at no later date in his career did he show any trait of character, or express any opinion, or act from any point of view, which he had not made us all familiar with as students. He had the deposit which makes certain cranks the salt of the earth and was, I imagine, a crank by inheritance. I never heard him speak of his family but his father, I have always understood, was a somewhat 'contrairy' man who, being himself an Inspector of Schools under the Board of National Education and a graduate of the Royal College of Science, knew more about education than most people. Accordingly, he sent his son to no school, or at least to no secondary school, but taught him at home. Skeffington's matriculation to the Royal University in the summer of 1896 is recorded as being after 'private study', and entering University College he brought with him the concentrated intelligence that was likely in such circumstances. His behaviour seemed to be regulated in accordance with long-settled opinions privately arrived at. All his movements were rapid and decisive. He thought, talked and walked rapidly. One never saw him loafing or doing anything at random. He could be still over a chess board, and could play blindfold two or three simultaneous games; any time I happened to be one of his adversaries he invariably won. He played no other games, did not swim, and keen though he was on walking and cycling he did not expatiate at large; his briskness appeared to be dictated by either a hygienic or a missionary purpose. He had principles on health as on everything else; wore Jaeger and homespuns like

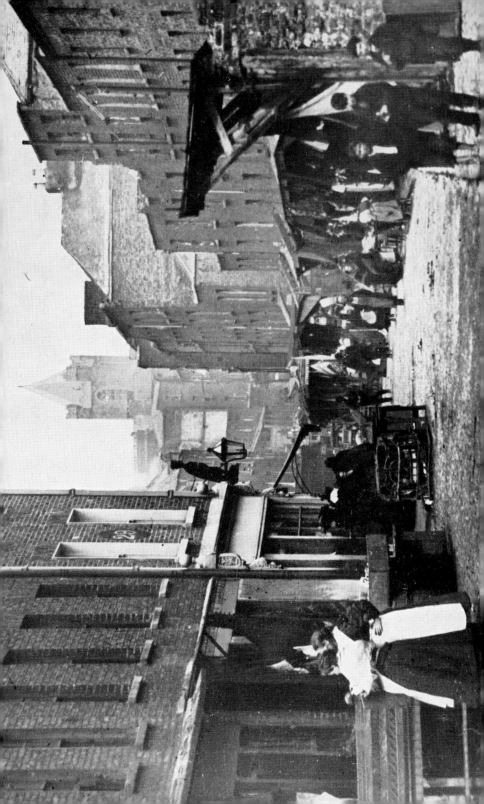

Bernard Shaw and his beard as prophylactic for a delicate throat. It goes, therefore, without saying that he was a teetotaller, a vegetarian and a non-smoker. These were days when in London the Eustace Miles restaurants mixed moral principles with dietetic statistics on their depressing menu cards and the same atmosphere pervaded the old Vegetarian restaurant in College Street. It took a good deal of courage on Skeffington's part to carry these airs into student life, but he did so. After his comparatively early marriage, I remember a large party he gave his student friends from which at a certain moment we were all thrown out of his house and given a quarter of an hour to smoke in the garden before plunging back to our talk indoors.

Skeffington always stood on his common law rights while regarding everything that was conventional as a challenge that demanded his scrutiny. Loving argument, he had a set opinion on every point of human behaviour; at an age when students are content to hold many opinions in solution, his were all armed *cap à pied* and ready for battle. His every opinion was a principle for which he was ready to die. As an officer of the L. & H., for example, having to discuss the general protocol of a special meeting with the president of the College, the discussion proceeded towards its friendly close. But Skeffington, with his fixed opinion on rational dress, was wearing his knickerbockers as usual and Father Delany ventured to say that on this evening he should wear the dress proper to gentlemen on such an occasion. In his staccato Ulster accent Skeffington said 'I shall come as I am or not at all.' And accordingly, he did not come. Being satisfied in his own mind that the L. & H. had no authority under its rules to subscribe to an Irish Language fund he resigned from the Society. He was present at the meeting which founded the Cui Bono—a club of some twelve college students bound in close intimacy. We were, I believe, all feminists but we did not propose easily to extend our number. When it appeared that we were not forthwith going to exemplify the principle of equality

H

of the sexes by an immediate election, he promptly resigned his membership.

In the teeth of Joseph de Maistre, Skeffington was at any time ready to die not merely for truth but for any truth. He translated every belief he had into action and lived at its indecorous extreme, forcing it on your attention by its evident incongruity with circumstance. If his view of justice was at odds with actual conditions so much the worse for things as they were. He narrowed his fighting front in the course of time to two issues: suffrage and labour, but without much change in his propagandist tactics. In student days, his principles, exercised over too wide a ground, quickly lost their novelty. His positions in debate were all automatically assumed; his lively offensives were relished but taken for granted and his logic, like most logic, shut out more wisdom that it unlocked. His favourite assaults were upon Gaelic Leaguers, bishops and conservatives. The controversies he so stirred up were rarely without a grain of reason. That they lacked a sense of proportion and were, as often as not, trivial did not trouble him. Impervious to ridicule, never known to be angry, they were part of his system of provocative tactics which he believed opened the way to cool reason. Tactics was his invariable defence of what to the rest of us was plainly absurd. 'Tactics' was a word often on his lips and the sound of it as he pronounced it, staccato and challenging, still brings his personality before me. But, whatever he hoped from the reasonable milieu in which we found ourselves, I never knew him in those days to modify any opinion. It was both his and our loss that for all their modernity his ideas and attitudes were stereotyped. Intercourse with him had no unexpected attraction. He showed, to be sure, more warmth and friendliness in private relations, but no new facets.

When I first knew him he was reading for his Master's degree in the modern language course in which he had graduated. In one way it was a curious choice. With his political and journalistic bent one would have expected to find him on the political economy or history side. Though he loved the theatre and from the beginning of the new theatre movement was a regular first nighter, he had little concern for literature outside its social content; elected auditor of the L. & H. it was almost a matter of course that his address to the society should be on *Realism in Fiction*. He had no enthusiasm for poetry and was indifferent to style save for the effective presentation of argument. Meredith he admired more I should think for his social criticism and attitude towards women than for his briary wit. I have his copy of *Diana of the Crossways* amongst my books. He followed every word of it with his pencil, underscoring each line with impulsive assiduity and with an overflow into the margins of admiring or exclamatory markings. Wholly extrovert in his talk I felt in him little or no sense of the supernatural, no interest in philosophy or metaphysics and he was as deaf to music as he was blind to the visual arts. On the one occasion when he was seen in the Louvre he was lifting no eye to its walls but was quick-stepping its galleries to verify, he said, Baedeker's statement that merely to walk through them took two hours. In this, he was own brother to a Hungarian journalist I once met in the Leaning Tower of Pisa—he was counting the steps—and to one of our early nineteenth-century judges, a master of minute erudition, who loving mathematical detail, knew the number of paces he took from his house in Merrion Square to the Four Courts.

A radical and democrat in the tradition of John Stuart Mill, Skeffington at college was a devout reader of *The Review of Reviews*. He adopted to his own purpose some of W. T. Stead's exhibitionist tactics but without that editor's pomposity. In Irish affairs Michael Davitt was his single admiration and in public matters Davitt's outlook was at this period most like to his own. Like Davitt he was a luke-warm Parliamentarian counting Westminster subordinate to more militant action on the home ground. He took the side of labour and democracy in college discussions and was feminist in everything. In our other domestic quarrels he was secularist in the Irish sense of the term and retrospectively anti-Parnellite. How opposed he was in this to his friend, James Joyce, who admiring Parnell for his proud self-containment also held him the victim of disloyalty. Skeffington judged Parnell cold, conservative, and, before and after Committee Room 15, disingenuous. He wrote him down as a political opportunist and the merely eponymous hero of the movement. These anti-Parnellite views may seem at variance with Skeffington's anti-clericalism but only to those who want to see the Parnell controversy simply as a clerical and anti-clerical faction fight. They forget that with Michael Davitt it was the English episcopophagi and secularists, the Rev. Hugh Price Hughes, W. T. Stead and John Morley, who were first in the anti-Parnellite field.

Skeffington and Joyce were always good friends, however much the publicist deplored the artist's seclusion. Joyce made play with Skeffington-McCann college propaganda but it is worth noting that even though Joyce was a completely unpolitical Parnellite he makes no reference to Skeffington's anti-Parnellism nor to Skeffington's adherence to the students' protest on the occasion of the first performance of Yeats's *The Countess Cathleen*. For Joyce to introduce either detail into his writing would put his *Portrait* out of drawing. Joyce's commentators show the same selective silence. Wisely perhaps. The parrots could not otherwise cry in tune. Though Skeffington's methods in controversy were summary and over-simplified, fairness was one of his salient and most honourable characteristics. His fugitive *Dialogues of the Day,* continued in his *National Democrat,* show the debater's capacity for entering into an opponent's point of view. It is all the more regrettable that, living on occasional journalism, he has left behind him no independent writing sufficiently self-contained to be taken as an apologia. His one substantial book, his *Life of Michael Davitt,* written in 1908, is a very incomplete and unsatisfactory performance, an extended essay rather than biography, but *faute*

de mieux it does light up the writer's character in his noting of
what he finds admirable in his subject. He finds in him freedom
from the spirit of hate; a nationalism that was uncompromisingly
democratic and, as he thinks, necessarily anti-clerical; a democrat-
ism that sought the elimination of the very poor and the very
rich and shied away from socialism as threatening human liberty,
and, most significantly, a repugnance to all forms of political
opportunism, meaning by opportunism the readiness to betray
one principle to secure the triumph of another. Skeffington's
summing-up of Michael Davitt may be fairly taken to mirror
much of himself at that date though his growing identity with
labour drew him later, along with his friend Fred Ryan, into the
reconstituted Irish Socialist Republican party under the able
labour leader Bill O'Brien. He gave it his general support but
he could hardly be regarded as any Party's man or other than an
individualist restive when obliged to work in tandem.

His lonely initiative in the 1916 Insurrection led to his murder
by a British military authority and, following his death, he was
written of mainly as a pacifist. Skeffington was not a pacifist in
the Quaker or Tolstoyan sense. He was always mounting barri-
cades. He would not himself, I think, in any circumstances, have
taken up arms to kill; but in his *Life of Davitt,* written it is true
before the first World War, he quite definitely maintained that
'as long as the Fenians could perceive the smallest chance of a
successful issue (they) were I will not say justified but morally
bound to make an attempt at organized rebellion.' His physical
courage, remarkable in a man who was not very robust, was as
boundless as his moral courage. It brought him, over and over
again, at Suffrage meetings into violent collision with the bravoes
of the Ancient Order of Hibernians. He was ready to go into
action side by side with Liberty Hall when it was proposed to
seize and occupy the Mansion House in 1914 against the Asquith-
Redmond recruitment meeting. Sunday after Sunday he addressed
anti-recruitment meetings in Beresford Place until he was jailed.

In all this he acted from an expressly national standpoint and certainly not primarily from pacifism.

These seeds were stirring in his college days. Nationalist and democratic though almost all of us were, few agreed with his most characteristic opinions and none with the expression he then gave them. He was, as I have said, the cat-fish in our tank. Differing from him, we all loved him for his unfailing good temper in argument, his courage and his Cato-like intransigence. In the student body it was he with Tom Kettle who had the most vivid sense of actuality and of the responsibilities that go with our only gradually awakening social conscience.

Hugh Kennedy

Skeffington came into college with Arthur Clery in 1896, a year after Hugh Kennedy who had entered before matriculation. Kennedy like Skeffington had never attended any secondary school but had been coached by his father, Surgeon Hugh Boyle Kennedy, a Donegal man, who was well grounded in the classics and had some not inconsiderable knowledge of Irish. They lived in North Great Denmark Street, and as a schoolboy, like all the natives of that north side area, I was familiar with the appearance of our future Chief Justice, a chubby-faced boy returning on his pony in the afternoons from the Phoenix Park. They were, as I was to see later, a highly individualized family. The girls were charming and accomplished in their different ways. The eldest of them, Mary Olivia, I knew first when from Loreto College she was beginning to write, tartly and smartly, a Girl Graduates' page in *St Stephen's,* and later in London when she was lady correspondent of *The Times,* mondaine and sophisticated by reason of her job, witty and sharp-tongued with a touch of cynicism. She could laugh at herself at work and watched the development of her brother's career with an elder sister's amused interest, and with less surprise the vicissitudes of her younger brother, the idle apprentice, from his noisy and impetuous beginnings. Hugh must have read much in a solitary way when young, charting his course with precocious gravity. In college he had no intimates until he knit a close friendship with Arthur Clery. For a comparatively long time I watched him in the L. & H. without much personal contact. His appearance was somewhat unusual. He was always very neatly attired and even as a student dressed almost as a professional man. His smooth, rosy face was, one would say, untouched by a razor. His voice was then naturally high-pitched, clear and thin, but he would raise and lower it, striving for some oratorical effect. This deliberate purpose entered into his every appearance at the L. & H. His speeches seemed carefully prepared in an old-fashioned style as if he had studied Grattan and Cicero. He probably had. There was nothing spon-taneous or conversational in his addresses or anything approaching the vernacular. Everything was formal, polished and prepared but he escaped the platitudes which threaten this manner by the elegance of his diction and by the real conviction and logic of his argument. Neither did his set discourse nor formal delivery prevent him from being an excellent debator though he had nothing of Tom Kettle's epigrammatic wit or drive and he fell short of Arthur Clery's naturally graceful and witty urbanity. There was nothing unexpected in his approach, no capture by surprise, no passion, but in their place a persuasive moderation, unruffled clearness, good temper and good sense. His intervention in debate had, therefore, none of the sparkle of Kettle or Clery or the sparks that flew when Skeffington got up. Nor had he the lively readiness of John Marcus O'Sullivan who preferred to speak from the briefest of notes taken in the course of debate, relying solely on attack, never fully expressing or expounding his own basic position but jerking out pithy criticism of his opponent's. Hugh Kennedy's practice was both artificial and candid. It contrasted equally in manner with Louis Walsh whose views were in essentials not greatly different from his own.

I was presently to see much more of Hugh Kennedy in the

Cui Bono and at work in the Four Courts but I never saw any change in the extreme care for detail and the foresight that marked his early years. It marked his judgements in the Supreme Court just as the same sense of form marked his handwriting. Long familiar with its clear distinction I was not surprised to find him at the Bar insisting that a new *call* who sought to 'devil' with him when a junior should first take lessons from a writing master. As a student he used the L. & H. obviously as the palestra for his profession, but he first took lessons in elocution and though medals in due course came his way he was in no haste to seek auditorial honours. Skeffington and Tom Kettle almost inevitably became auditors in their second year at college, but Kennedy put off standing for that distinction until he had taken his honours degree in classics, and was finishing his legal course. In his year as auditor, constructive as Felix Hackett, with him he founded *St Stephen's*. He had joined the Gaelic League a year or two before and was a member of the Central Branch at the same time as John MacNeill, Pearse and Eamonn Kent. Later he was for a time its honorary secretary. He had probably picked up some Irish from his father but his knowledge of it in University College days was slight and his later Chancery work gave him small opportunity to extend it. It was characteristic of his tenacity that he did extend it. Interested in every aspect of Irish scholarship, he resumed its study when his public work was most arduous and, linking it with the rest, he gave it most effective expression as one of the framers of the Constitution and as Attorney General and Chief Justice.

It is not out of place that I should recall what my friend Professor Delargy told me. In the years when Delargy was an underpaid lecturer in the College and Hugh Kennedy Attorney General to the new State, he was engaged by him and Mr John M. Costello, to give them grinds in Irish. Characteristically, the only hour the Attorney General could fix for the purpose was 11 p.m. Sleep and the clock were to Kennedy always secondary considerations. Nature, he said, had so made him that he could sleep on the hearthrug. The grind went on to three o'clock in the morning. On Jack Costello's side the grind was at his only possible time, when walking to the Courts from Herbert Park.

Kennedy was a Redmondite and an orthodox Home Ruler who came late into touch with Sinn Fein. Wondering at this I asked Mr W. T. Cosgrave how the contact came about. He told me that in the first republican days, Kevin O'Higgins, as revolutionary Minister for Local Government, brought forward a stringent proposal to ensure the proper payment of rates. Mr Cosgrave thought it too harsh and perhaps unjust. He said he would take legal opinion on it and was recommended (I think by that good Nationalist and solicitor the late Michael Corrigan) to go to Hugh Kennedy whom he had never met. Mr Cosgrave and Kevin O'Higgins went to Kennedy's house in Waterloo Road. Kennedy read the proposed rule with obvious disapproval and said it was against 'natural justice' and should not be adopted. 'It was the first time,' Mr Cosgrave told me, 'I had heard the phrase "natural justice".'

It was following on this that Kennedy, on Mr Costello's advice, was briefed in the Egan *habeas corpus* case, his greatest success at the Bar. It was brought during the Black and Tan terror when he won from the Master of the Rolls, Charles O'Connor, the writ which stayed the operation of the British military courts in Ireland outside the martial law area. The case made history inasmuch as it was the first Irish instance in which on a capital charge the civil courts successfully restrained the operation of a military order, and the judgement of the Rolls stigmatizing the executives' conduct as 'red ruin and the breaking up of law' was a prologue to the treaty negotiations. It determined also the counsel's future career. He was made party to these negotiations and legal adviser to the new provisional government, and Attorney General in the new State, a framer of its Constitution, and its first Chief Justice. His share in the establishment of our

Department of Justice and of the Irish judicial system is now part of our history, and the new cables of the ship of state were of the same tough fibre as himself. The threads run back to University College and were perceptible in the quiet, unsensational, orderly and constructive progress of his student career. The moderation in the expression of his firmly held opinions and the patient, exact thoroughness with which he carried through all he then conceived and undertook hardly concealed his hidden ardour and the essential radicalism of his convictions. His religious belief was thoughtful and deep-seated; his education ran on classical lines, his mind open and responsive to the humane appeal of music and the visual arts. He belonged to a formal and conservative profession. With a wider and deeper culture he was more expressly nationalist than Skeffington and at the same time as democratic and modern in his outlook. As radical as Skeffington, his radicalism had its roots not in John Stuart Mill or in any English soil and when it came his way he faced the task of constitution making with his back turned to English models. When he sought outside guidance it was rather to America and Switzerland that he looked. At the close of my own college course I had been reading *The Federalist* and was not unfamiliar with the problems dealt with by Hamilton, Madison and Jay, and with the contribution made by Chief Justice Marshall to the constitution of the United States. Twenty years after, in his constitution-making days, I found him far more deeply conversant with their thought than I was and much more radical than they. When we were disentangling from the British connection, the legal profession as a whole were above all things anxious to preserve all that was possible of old forms and precedents. True to the motto on the King's Inns dining plate—*nolumus mutari*—our elders still hoped to carry on with the minimum change. The 'old gang' in the Law Library, however ready

> New gods to serve and with them yet,
> To get what there was left to get,

had, behind their own obsolescent and honourable loyalties, much timidity and an ingrained professional conservatism. They knew little of the quiet revolutionary in their midst and of the resolute thoroughness with which, supported by John O'Byrne and John Costello, his axe would be laid to their upas tree. That axe was ground not in Trinity but in University College, through which the Greenwich Meridian did not run. From the outset he gave full legal effect to the revolution won by arms, establishing a wholly new legal system. He placed it in right relation with the people by its efficient and modern structure, the elimination of all royal titles and pompous irrelevancies and by the use of the Irish language in the Courts. Republican and democrat, he had an unqualified admiration for Michael Collins. A warm and understanding friendship had grown up between the man of action and the man of law. It began with Hugh Kennedy's defence of the Republican prisoners which earned for the lawyer the respect and affection of Collins, always passionately loyal to his comrades-in-arms, and his confidence was confirmed during the Treaty negotiations and Kennedy's subsequent work on the Constitution.

When our dissensions had mounted to civil war Albert Beveridge's *Life of Chief Justice Marshall* appeared and I read with special interest the letters that passed between Washington, Jay and Madison at the period of Shayer's Rebellion and the civil disorders that threatened the very existence of the new States. Washington's letters were filled with profound gloom and disillusion. I copied some of them and sent them to Kennedy for the consolation of his colleagues and himself shut up in Government Buildings. Soon afterwards Kennedy told me he had taken them with him to Collins, then Commander-in-Chief of the Free State forces, when seeing him off at Kingsbridge Station on the journey that ended at Béal Átha Blath. To his astonishment he found Collins had with him for the journey a copy of the *Life of Marshall*. The story is true to Collins's range of mind. I link it with another indicating Collins's sound capacity as a literary critic. He once casually referred to Swinburne as 'that melodious oul' banjax'.

I have said that from his earliest days Kennedy was meticulous and he grew to care more for exactness in his work than for the clock. In a speech at a dinner of the Incorporated Law Society I heard its president chaff him on his delay in giving his reserved judgements and say that when they were on more equal footing he had to wait even longer for his written opinions, 'But when the opinion came it was worth having.' When he was Attorney General I have heard that a Minister did equally repine of a bottle-neck department into which files flowed freely and rarely emerged. The day came when Hugh was appointed Chief Justice and he gave a sherry party before leaving the Attorney General's office. Amongst his guests was Gordon Campbell, Secretary to Industry and Commerce. Campbell went over to the office safe, carefully and meditatively examined it until Kennedy came over to ask him what he was doing with his safe. Campbell said he always understood it was not a safe but some sort of sluice that piped Industry and Commerce files to an outflow beyond the Liffey Pigeon House.

Regardless of time, unsparing in his labour and simple in his tastes, he was especially careful to maintain the appropriate dignity of the Bench free from sham. Easy of access, he was scrupulous in observing the decorum of great office. Except perhaps in one point. More or less immured in Government Buildings during our civil fighting, he kept an old taxi driver in his service who took risks with him when out in an ancient Ford. He retained his services in peace-time and the old Ford lay at all hours outside the Chief Justice's Court in the Upper Castle Yard. An American tourist saw it there and remarked on its appearance. He was told it was the Chief Justice's car. 'Some democratic Chief Justice,' said the American.

Arthur Clery

Contemporary with Hugh Kennedy in U.C.D. was his class fellow, Arthur Clery—another future judge, but in his case a judge of the Sinn Féin courts.

My mind likes to dwell on Arthur Clery, that modest lovable man, not for his legal ability, for it was in no way exceptional, nor for any trace he left on public affairs, for, except by way of example, he left none, nor for his virtues and they were many, but for a quiet contrariness that teased, tantalized and fascinated his friends and for a riddling element in his make-up that turned him aside from well-trodden ways into private retreats of his own. Except that it was unpredictable, I am wrong in calling this disturbing factor riddling and would be equally wrong if I should suggest it is to be found in many saints. Clery in fact was or became an obstinate idealist, but less practical than Skeffington and cast in a different mould, though his singularity did not appear in his student years. In those years he was very fairly representative of University College in its temper, teaching and student reaction to the outside world, but they belied his later development. When he succeeded Tom Kettle as auditor of the L. & H. he seemed to me to be groomed for an inevitable professional success at the Bar. It is true that Joyce wrote of him then slightingly as 'the college orator, a most amenable young man who spoke at all meetings'. It was, after all, his duty to do so. Joyce's sharp eye was not at fault in detecting in him an occasional nervous mannerism. But this was in *Stephen Hero* which Joyce did his best to destroy as a schoolboy production. Clery spoke to Joyce's two papers at the L. & H. and in friendly though critical fashion. Beyond this they had no contact. His reading was in the ancient classics and otherwise mainly in the august period of the eighteenth century. Devoted to the theatre, he had then the routine admirations which Joyce rejected; he identified Ibsen with the problem play and deplored both. This was the normal attitude of 1898. As auditor he was graceful, suave and winning; his good manners were unfailing. The little *éloges* with which he concluded the society's meetings with neatly turned compliments to chairman and speakers were accomplished performances in that urbane art. His formal speeches were in the manner of his favourite eighteenth century and rose in unforced seemliness superior to eloquence. Sanity was packaged in good taste and seasoned with wit. His sentences fell in impeccable, expected cadence and were pointed by a pleasing gift of epigram. He retained two of his papers from this youthful 1898–99 period in his *Dublin Essays* collected and published twenty years later. One is entitled 'Irish Genius in English Prose'; the other deals with the theatre, and though he recants in a footnote some of the opinions of this first essay, finding it full of the cocksureness of youth, too loyal to received opinion and with too little awareness of the poetic revival about him, they are for this very reason worth looking into as a picture of a normal collegian of the date coming from a good school and interested in the stage. He makes polite obeisance to the Gaelic language revival, wishes it well, finding in Gaelic poetry the embodiment of the Irish soul. Like John Eglinton's modern Irishman he perfunctorily saluted Gaelic literature while proudly recognizing that the true expression of Irish genius was in our eighteenth-century prose. He stood cheering on the sidewalk while Swift, Burke, Goldsmith and Sheridan went by, leading captive the conquering English tongue. He modelled his style on the English nineteenth century but was determined by the Greeks and Latins and by Christian humanism. He loved the living theatre and—if more than a little prudish—he was not insular. In these early papers and college debates he reprobates Ibsen as I have said, knows what Pinero is doing and what the Frenchmen meditate but, steered by Sophocles and Shakespeare, keeps an even keel. It is in their name he rejects the fallacy that the stage should be a teaching force. It should not be didactic; it should amuse, affect and elevate and so he deprecates the problem-play, 'the product of dilute Ibsenism'. He finds Coppée and Rostand more admirable than the Pinero plays with which George Alexander held the boards. He has the foresight in 1898 to anticipate some new and more splendid era for the Irish theatre. His name is not amongst the signatories to the college students' protest against *The Countess Cathleen*.

It looked to me at this time, knowing nothing of his slender resources and lonely youth, as if every wind was conspiring to favour an auspicious course towards some safe haven in the legal profession upon which he was entering. But it was at this moment when discretion pointed to the path that led to a County Court judgeship that he encountered the Gaelic serum which had begun to run through the college. His new outlook upon national affairs was allied to his interest in the university agitation. Becoming a regular contributor to D. P. Moran's newly founded *Leader* he found in it and in *The New Ireland Review* and in *Studies* congenial outlets for his opinions.

Writing was in fact his true mètier. Conscientiously, through these *Dublin Essays* we can trace him until he stands, bare and unashamed, for the integral Ireland of the Gaelic League. With his graduate's gown he put aside the things of English culture, kept nothing of the eighteenth century but its love of an epigram and now with inquisitive mind and obstinate irritating questionings he set out on a Socratic journey through Irish society. His quest was the native Irishman. The ideal proportions of that good citizen are present to his mind but when he applies the tape measure to *homo hibernicus* and calls out the accusatory inches we feel the Socratic indiscretion. There are things that should not be mentioned outside the 'trying-on room'—that slight fulness about the waist; those unpleasing assymetries; maybe an undue curvature of the spine. He sets them all down, and this is the virtue of his writing—that the reader may overhear, if only as from a conversation in the next room, Arthur Clery's talk with his friends in the Cui Bono. He wrote then as he talked, with

127

cheerful candour and wit, without any messianic zeal. If he has to consider Ireland from the denominational angle he does not find it appropriate to marshal the figures of the Protestant counties or to tick off factory-chimneys against spires and round towers. He prefers to count the dinners he has eaten at Protestant houses and the Protestant girls he has danced with. He knows that his partner knows that her mother and herself are wasting their time and tea and cakes on a plainly unmarriageable man. From such knowledge he builds up his image of Irish society, a society where, in general, the coincidence of religion and politics had established two self-sufficing circles rotating on independent axes.

I have elsewhere recalled a college Inaugural, a formal occasion and one of some importance since it heralded a new phase in the university quarrel and the platform was graced with the presence of Augustine Birrell. Birrell's speech was charged with the usual expressions of sympathy and with promises with which we were too familiar. On this occasion, as events proved, there was reality in the pledges, but it availed Birrell nothing. It was then that Arthur Clery spoke as no one since J. F. Taylor had spoken on a university platform. The unexpected ferocity of his speech was enhanced by a shaggy beard which in this period of revolt from the conventions, Arthur, temporarily, chose to wear. Do I exaggerate when I say that he rent, flayed, tore and tattered that well-meaning Chief Secretary? He made that platform of stuffed shirts look like some arena where a bewildered bull staggered staring, uncomprehending, under a rain of darts. Yes, he scrapped his formal eloquence and received ideas with his graduate's gown; scrapped too what looked like a career and became a new man. From that day on he lived an Irish Aristides, entirely unworldly living on the point of honour, and as some would say, quixotically.

At any rate, writing was his true métier. However admirable a speaker and later as Professor of Law—a part-time post in the new University—he was not, in truth, fitted for the Bar. He had a discursive intellectual interest in law but nothing of the forceful concentration, the absorbing, relentless fanaticism of its votaries. And so from his seat in the Law Library from the early 1900s he watched the jockeying for place which he despised and the healthier competition and argle-bargle for which he was temperamentally unfitted. A junior himself, with gentle but growing irony he played mentor to his own juniors in the worldly wisdom he was without. He would have been happier, as his friend Willie Dawson wrote, as a university don for he loved to be with students. More and more he found life most agreeable in the society of young students or in wandering here and there over Ireland. But he never forsook our club, the Cui Bono, where Kettle loved his sallies and Chestertonian paradoxes. When I sought from Chief Justice Kennedy a date for our meeting that would fit into his public engagements his only query was to ascertain that Arthur would surely be there. Kettle called him our Goldsmith and there was some reason for it. Clery had his own way of thinking and there was depth under its apparent simplicity.

Why is it that from all our duels of wit and out of all our talks and walks, music and theatre-going, one remembers a most lovable presence certainly but, more than his wit, his mannerisms and oddities? On foreign excursions he would attempt any language, including Latin, rather than be taken for an Englishman, but why should he insist at some impossible moment in a Bierhaus on inordinate supplies of milk or tea? Or at home why should he ape the Frenchman and tuck his dinner napkin under his chin? Why not, he might say, it is unreasonable to do otherwise. And why the restlessness that made him only 'look in' at parties, going everywhere, staying long nowhere. It was not that like Chaucer's lawyer he wished to seem busier than he was. Did he see himself the detached spectator of vanity fair or was it that, as one cheated of fuller experience, he was driven to pass in one evening from a drawing-room to a committee-meeting, a rowing club, and a

I

céilidh dance? He would have liked to excel in games but did not. Growing rotund, he practised as a physical exercise—singing, unfortunately likewise. In the gods, as a student, comforted with grapes, he loved the opera; ever afterwards his soul found within itself the makings of a Caruso. The expressionist maestro was a challenge to him and he took singing lessons by stealth. Thereafter he would at any moment abuse his own voice and the ears of friends by singing the parts of Isolde as well as Tristan from end to end. He was as assiduous in his attempts to master Irish, but he himself owned that he had achieved only *blas gan Gaedhilge*. He read closely rather than widely, looking for provocative fodder, and he handled books with a masterly indifference that rivalled Skeffington's. The disorder in which he kept his books and music was complete, but when I reproached him once for this unprincipled arrangement of his shelves, his retort was equally complete, 'What do you mean?' he said. 'They are in perfect order. I arrange my books according to their owners.'

He kept his neatness for epigrams: 'One difference', he said, 'between Ireland and England is that in England you can say what you like as long as you don't do it. In Ireland you can do what you like as long as you don't say it.' I do not agree with his account of the split of the Treaty—that de Valera captured the I.R.A. and Collins the I.R.B.—but the Law Library concurred, as it seldom did, with his opinion that 'a judge of first instance should be quick, courteous and generally wrong'. I am told that his law lectures covered conscientiously the Law of Property but they were informal and conversational. He defined a contingent remainder as the chance to a dispensary doctor's son to inherit the dispensary. Characteristic in another sphere was his description of a University sermon he heard at the beginning of term. Defining the frontiers of theology and science it too often happened that some cliché-ridden preacher would bear ponderously on what was invariably called pseudo-science. An occasion came

when Arthur was pleased and he expressed his satisfaction as
Tacitus might have done. *Enituit, sermo* he said, *bello intacto,
scientia integra.* (The sermon excelled in this that the war was not
alluded to and the customary attack on science was absent.)

The wrecking of the Home Rule Bill, the war and the events
of 1916 ended his more indulgent reveries and speculations. Was
it typical, or the accident of circumstance, that himself, Kettle
and Fitzgerald-Kenney alone of the Cui Bono joined the Irish
Volunteers? But when John Redmond flung discord into the
movement with his Woodenbridge speech and the split came,
Kettle and Fitzgerald-Kenney sided with Redmond while Clery
went with MacNeill and Pearse. In this contrary action of Kettle
and Clery, two men equally high-minded, there was more than
the easy antithesis between politician and idealist. They were
both idealists in their fashion. Kettle's decision and his death at
Ginchy were in character and congruous with the impulse which
had committed him immediately and irrevocably. His political
judgement and his party-loyalty ran together. Admirable as it
was to see Clery an Irish Volunteer in arms, yet to see him as a
soldier made some smile, however shame-facedly. I cannot help
thinking that an old polarization was at work and that Kettle's
example contributed to fling Clery's gears the more violently
into reverse with some incongruity, not with his convictions but
with his appearance and outward nature. The circumstances of
the Easter Rising withheld him from the G.P.O. but his courage
was never in question. He was counsel for the defendant at
MacNeill's court martial. Presently Clery became a Supreme
Court judge in the Sinn Féin Court—by accident, not its president. He might have been Chief Justice in those revolutionary
days. Austin Stack, then Minister for Home Affairs, had intended
him for that post. But Austin Stack, as Collins wrathfully knew,
was not a very efficient administrator. When the Minister came
to the room where Clery and his two intended judicial colleagues,
James Creed Meredith and Diarmuid O'Crowley, met for their

inauguration and first sitting, Stack dilly-dallied, standing about in unnecessary conversation until James Creed Meredith calmly said, 'Well, I suppose I had better sit here,' and there he remained as head of the Court. Arthur never told me that story but years later when I asked him how James Creed arrived to that position he simply said, 'James Creed was a good runner.' Meredith, in fact, when a student in T.C.D. had held an All Ireland Championship for the quarter mile.

Clery took the anti-Treaty side and as such was elected one of his University's representatives to Dáil Éireann in 1927. In common with his party he abstained from taking his seat by reason of the oath imposed by the Treaty and so far as he could he ignored the institutions of the new State. He did not accept nomination at any subsequent Dáil election. When de Valera changed his attitude in regard to the oath and entered the Dáil and eventually into government, Clery stubbornly refused to follow him; he continued to live, however quixotically, on the point of honour. Disillusioned, he was gradually withdrawing from every form of public activity. After the Treaty his colleagues on the republican Bench had gone their separate ways; one to his place in the now Free State High Court; another departed to the south of France on his pension as a republican judge and wrote lengthy letters to the papers against the new Constitution. Clery went back to his seat in the Law Library. As a former judge he declined to appear before the new tribunals but he also refused to draw his judicial pension and, refusing at the same time to fill up any income tax statement since he did not admit the new Revenue authority, was mulcted accordingly.

By this time, Aristides might have become Diogenes but Clery was too fine a Christian for the cynic's tub though the pessimistic streak in him became more evident. He grew reticent and pessimism coloured his conversation. It became an amalgam of oblique observation and tart humour. Frustrated idealism had, however, the indefeasible backing of conduct. A celibate, he lived with

quietly fierce independence, caring as little for the general opinion
as for money. He lived deliberately poor on his slender salary as
a part-time professor, and yet generously—more generous in his
actions than in his judgements. St Francis de Sales wrote: '. . . on
ne perd rien à vivre genéreusement, noblement, courtoisement et
avec un coeur, loyal, égal et raisonnable'. Arthur read the last
adjective his own way.

He was in fact something of an anarchist, something of a saint,
something of a La Rochefoucauld. Irony is the natural shield of the
idealist. Clery's irony was itself more and more eaten into by the
pessimism which, already present in his writing in 1910, invaded
his talk and crept even into his lectures. George Moore wrote
somewhere that the spark of genius dies out at thirty and the fire
must be kept going by talent. However true this may be in the
arts—though it is discounted by his own case and pre-eminently
by his contemporaries, the Yeatses—Clery had a similar view of
political morality. He must, I think, be a dangerous guide to youth
who denies honesty to public men after forty. Yet, public honesty,
Clery would maintain, was the quality of the early twenties and
voting should be restricted to that age. It survived later only in a
few men, he would admit, like Davitt who had their principles
preserved in the antiseptic atmosphere of a British gaol. He quoted
Lord Russell of Killowen who defended his own emigration on
the ground that most of the men he had seen succeed in Ireland
were mean men. Russell, he said, saw that the successful man and
the good citizen were in Ireland almost opposed and, continued
Clery, on further analysis he would probably have found the
Irishman's alternatives to be treachery, poverty or emigration.
This, I hasten to say, was in 1910 and it was the sort of provocation
he liked to give the Cui Bono just as with greater justice he would
say that the Irishman who would write for posterity must write
for export. Provocative merely or not, Clery could never in his
heart reconcile success with good citizenship. His too easy acceptance of defeat for the good citizen was a premonitory symptom

133

K

of his own failure to leave a deeper mark on his generation and in this he was unlike his friends Kettle and Pearse.

The Cui Bono

It was in the Cui Bono Club that Arthur Clery incubated most of his writing. The Cui Bono was an extra-mural grouping of a few college intimates who, even when undergraduates, had consolidated what proved to be lasting friendships. As post-graduates, still avid for discussion, we met, as students do everywhere, to listen to each other's papers and to put the universe in its place. Meeting first in cafés where a room could be had and a shilling went a long way, the advancing years transformed us into a dining club until death, reducing our members to a sad minority, changed our mirth to threnodies, our dinners to dirges.

Our name came to us from a much earlier generation, from a different C.U.I. Club of Newman's Catholic University which had on its committee in the 'seventies, George Sigerson and John Dillon. We survived all civil strife and differences of opinion. In our good years we were fourteen and none was without some particular quality. A majority were lawyers; all were versatile and none selfishly engrossed and none was without some distinction in philosophy, science, medicine, law, literature, politics or banking. We could count amongst our number two future Ministers in a yet unborn state—Ministers for Education and Justice, the first Chief Justice and another Supreme Court judge of the Irish Free State, a Supreme Court judge of the Sinn Féin Courts and indeed an acting Chief Justice *in partibus* in Burma. We had members of two legislatures and a future President of the Royal Dublin Society. Most of us were at one time or another doubling up our parts as professors and practitioners in our different avocations. As a group we had from the beginning many feelers out and like the centipede we were happy in our ditch asking which leg went after which but not selfishly or overmuch considering how to run.

Built around Tom Kettle and Arthur Clery, the Cui Bono barely survived their loss. They were its opposite poles. We felt each was conscious of his temperamental opposite, or since both had their unfortunate share of pessimism should one more correctly say that they were uneasily conscious of a climatic difference. Both had their hearts and feet in Ireland, but one looked towards Europe for salvation, the other inwards towards Ballingeary? Between them Willie Dawson sparked gaily with John Marcus O'Sullivan an equable centre of gravity.

Dawson had also been an auditor of the L. & H. but his friendship with Clery went back to earlier years when the Dawson house was wide open to the friendless schoolboy. It was Clery's association with *St Stephen's* and *The Leader* that in due course drew Dawson into writing. As *Avis* in these two papers he was a witty commentator on the passing show. In the little world of *St Stephen's,* he sparkled, protesting all the time, like the clown who would play Hamlet, that he wanted to write about his soul. A pretty anthology of wit with a special appeal to old stagers could be made from his lightly turned off journalism and from the squibs and topical verse in which he excelled. But his true quality was in the verve and acuteness of his talk, and it was at its best in the Cui Bono where he was wholly at ease. There was always something vivid and birdlike about him and his wit made swift arabesques around Clery's challenges and Kettle's broody response. His common sense had wings on helmet and heels. He delighted in Shaw and Wilde but his intelligence was independent of book-learning; it darted and wheeled, like Jimmy Montgomery's, with unexpected turns of witty phrase. Essentially metropolitan, he whistled and sang as a blackbird in the feathers of a town sparrow. He stood for the town against the country, against Fitzgerald-Kenney our landowner and against any conventional rural bias; deriding provincialism and dreading its incursion. He loved urban civilization anywhere but most of all in Dublin, his queen-city. He found ample play for his squibs and sallies within the ambit of Stephen's Green, and the Squares, the Arts Club and the theatre. He saw to it that no *wanderlust* should afflict him with boredom such as tore at the heart of a Royal Irish Constabulary man I once met in Kerry. That individual drifted down to me, lonely as a cloud, one morning as I sat on a wall eating my sandwich near the Musgrave police barracks above Killarney. I ventured to observe to him that it was a fine place. 'Ah, sir,' said he, 'it is a fine place to be passing through.' While his friends took every opportunity to range where they could from Aran to Athens and from the Lug (Lugnaquilla) to the Gross Glockner Dawson kept a Johnsonian indifference to such meanderings. If he ever left his city's 'fringes', it was as a student of human nature to observe its queer manifestations in Brighton or Blackpool, or even Paris. He linked that study with an inherited insight into politics. His father had sat in Westminster as one of Parnell's old party but was more widely known as Lord Mayor and Town Clerk of Dublin, a very familiar figure in its streets. Alert and spruce, impeccably dressed, flower in buttonhole, the elder Dawson delighted in an old-fashioned eloquence and in his own. From him, no doubt, came Willie's addiction to politics. He loved its backstage details and was steeped not only in the minutiae of Parnellite lore but in all the interwoven convolutions of nineteenth-century British politics. He knew its deeps and shallows and instinctively gauged their proportion. As sensitively as Tom Kettle's or Arthur Clery's, the needle of his mind felt the pull of every force. More accurately perhaps than either, it pointed their direction. I recall his parody of *The Croppy Boy* which was his quick and sharp answer to John Redmond's lamentable recruiting speech at Woodenbridge. I passed on the *MSS.* of these verses to Arthur Griffith on the next Saturday at the bookcarts in Aston's Row. Griffith printed them in his weekly and within a fortnight, to the writer's distress, a ballad singer got fourteen days in gaol for singing them at Macroom fair. Differing in 1914 from Kettle on the question of recruiting, he differed later from Clery on the Treaty issue, but his clear understanding was so free from party spirit and his loyalty in friendship so unswerving that his intimacy with both remained unclouded to the end.

No reasoning being could fail to appreciate Dawson's wit and enjoy his society. He was salt to any man's dish and most specially to an ingrained conservative as was Fitzgerald-Kenney, who was as I have said, our only landowner; the low moss-green walls of his Mayo property ran not far from Moore Hall, the property of his friend, Colonel Moore, on the enchanting, reed-fringed shores of Lough Carra. More papist than the Pope, Fitzgerald-Kenney also took amongst us the part of a Whig for which his out-of-the-way acquaintance with the lives of Lord Chancellors and eighteenth-century politics peculiarly fitted him. Not that he had any English affinities; his loyalties were to Edmund Burke and to Connacht. Born out of his age, he was younger than his appearance, with his tawny hair and eyebrows and steady, scrutinizing eyes he looked a ravaged Dante. His manner of speech was deliberately old-fashioned and seemed to carry its accent from the Regency. All his 'r's' were 'w's' as resolute as those of Chris Micks, his fellow-circuiter on the Connacht circuit. Once on circuit he was defending a poacher charged with the killing of a gamekeeper. Fitz presented the unfortunate result of the affair as a free-for-all outside a pub. 'Tell me,' he asked the R.I.C. sergeante 'wasn't this just a chance melée?' The sergeant was a stranger to the word and puzzled. Fitzgerald-Kenney encouraged him, 'Wasn't it only a mere "wumpus"?' The experienced sergeant still halted in his evidence. Chris Micks for the prosecution came to the rescue, 'Counsel means wasn't this a wow?'

His first paper in the Cui Bono, published afterwards in the *Contemporary Review,* was on devolution. If he did coquet with Dunraven's devolution it was not for long for in 1914 with Colonel Moore he was an officer in the western command of the National Volunteers, and one of its Inspectors. At all times he

delighted in opposing the grey language of experience to our
untested radicalism, and his realistic Mayoman's knowledge of
the countryside to the townsman's conception of the peasant.
Here, however, he met his match in Kettle.

We had another future Free State Minister in John Marcus
O'Sullivan who was called from his chair of history in University
College to take charge of Education during the same administration in which Fitzgerald-Kenney served as Minister for Justice.
He succeeded John MacNeill as Minister for Education in 1926.
O'Sullivan followed his natural bent for philosophy and he
finished his post-graduate course with distinction under Windel-
band in Heidelberg. While there he had been the planner and
pivot of our early walking tours in Switzerland and Austria. Back
home, for the Cui Bono he was as I have said the genial point of
rest between Kettle and Clery. His capacious mind comprehended
everything, reconciling, distinguishing and rejecting propositions
with a tolerant humour that overcame his instinctive impatience
with fallacious argument. In his early days in the college L. & H.
he liked to speak late in the proceedings and impromptu. He
preferred quick-fire demolition work to any elaborate exposition.
Later in Dáil Éireann, whether in or out of office, he lost nothing
of his dialectical agility but his genial equanimity in the face of
deceptive clichés was more manifest and made him a general
favourite. He had taken history in Germany as a *Nebenstudie* in
his doctoral course, and it was not wholly a misfortune that early
university politics had forced him to accept the chair of history
rather than the chair of philosophy he sought. Rooted in ortho-
doxy and with full knowledge of the ditches on either side of the
road he ever kept centre right in politics though wholly democratic in outlook. His first concern was to keep steady the newly
launched ship of state. He was impatient when abstractions invaded politics; he hated doctrinaires, if hate at that point could
enter his make-up; he was distrustful of novelty. He might rightly

be thought conservative but it should be remembered that it was during his tenure of office that Ingram's planning of vocational education was first given effect to in an Act.

Then there was Felix Hackett, the physicist and our expert in science, whom I have so far barely mentioned. He filled other high and honorary offices with equal credit—in the Royal Dublin Society of which he was Hon. Secretary and later President; in An Óige and the Royal Irish Academy, in the Dublin Institute for Advanced Studies, the National Library, and the Libraries Association. He also honourably discharged the functions of purse-bearer to the Cui Bono at home and to our walking tours abroad. His fellow member and townsman James Murnaghan doubled up the parts of Supreme Court judge and Chairman of the Governors of the National Gallery. I set down his name with equal affection for he seems to me to be the embodiment of that character in legal fiction known as the reasonable man who does all things with all the circumspection required by the law books; or almost all. He mixed valour with discretion in the Alps and in the auction rooms and picture dealers' shops. Together we made our first acquaintance of the Paris Galleries. Retaining his college-days' admiration for Greek art, he passed with careful steps into the eighteenth century until at last he retreated to his best loved haven amongst the Italian primitives. Far beyond the eighteenth century I could not tempt him—not even in opera. In those early days we shared, as we still do, an unqualified love for *The Marriage of Figaro* but my unprincipled taste admitted *Tristan* to an equal hearing. Night after night for our first fortnight in Paris we endured the hard seats of the Opéra Comique, often walking the long way back to our lodging in the Rue d'Assas. But never could I reconcile him to Wagner. He barely tolerated the Impressionists. Picasso and Braque were anathema to him. He belonged to the conservative wing of the Cui Bono where such diverse seeds manifested themselves. Nor would I willingly omit mention of a third Ulsterman not from Omagh but from Ballinascreen. Seamus O'Kelly was our nearest approach to an Irish native speaker. His grandmother, with whom he spent much of his boyhood, lived in one of the even then rare pockets of native Irish speakers which have now virtually disappeared. He was therefore our authority on Irish and indeed ran a class for some of us. He lived out his days as a doctor though I think he was not cut out for a professional career. He was not a Volunteer, probably by reason of his medical studies, but was in touch with the movement. Anticipating Joyce's portmanteau words a farmer-neighbour of his called him a 'contricate' man. He loved and fastened on minutiae and I could imagine him attaching at least equal importance to the dialect of his grandmother's parish as to Irish as a whole and the genealogy of an Irish family to Irish history. Devotion to minutiae leads to differences. He had a fine but limited taste in poetry, particularly in French poetry and more particularly in the poets of the *Pléiade* whom we read together with Joyce in class in University College. He had been to Paris for a short spell before coming to the college and we listened with interest to his amalgam of the Belfast and Parisian accent. I count it to my credit that I backed his successful attempts to translate into Irish at that time some lyrics from Marot and the *Pléiade* and at least one from Verlaine.

I make little mention here of Joyce of whom I have already written at greater length.[1] It is worth observing, however, in spite of repetition, that with the exception of Skeffington, neither in the *Portrait of an Artist* nor in *Stephen Hero* does Joyce dwell on any of these figures although they made the real atmosphere of University College where they were his contemporaries. The references he makes are but casual and have, including myself, been mistaken or confused by his commentators. I venture to assume that they are covered by a sentence in *Stephen Hero* where Joyce says that 'it must not be supposed that the popular University of Ireland lacked an intelligent centre'.

1. C. P. Curran, *James Joyce Remembered*, London 1968.

Kettle

Tom Kettle, under whose charm we all willingly lay, entered the college in 1897. His health was precarious and though he was a notable cyclist and cricketer in his schooldays and could later climb mountains and do his stint of twenty or twenty-five miles a day on our walking tours, ill-health interrupted his college terms and compelled him to retire at times to his father's farm at Artane and St Margaret's or to Innsbruck and Switzerland. If ill-health shadowed his life it also gave him an early and lasting acquaintance with continental life and thought. Even from a distance his magnetism drew us towards him and in post-graduate years John Marcus O'Sullivan came from Heidelberg, and Felix Hackett, James Murnaghan, Arthur Clery and myself from Dublin, to join him for expeditions in Tyrol, the Salzkammergut and the Bernese Oberland. His intellectual ascendancy was unquestioned and we recognized in him the most brilliant intelligence of our generation and its most widely and vigorously exercised mind.

I knew him first as my brother's contemporary at the O'Connell Schools, driving in each morning from his father's farm in North County Dublin. It was from his father he inherited both his realist sense of politics and its trenchant expression. His father was one of our earliest Land Reformers. He presided in 1879 at the meeting in the old Imperial Hotel in Sackville Street which founded the Land League and he was one of its honorary secretaries with Michael Davitt and Brennan. A clear thinking, hard-hitting man he was one of the few members of Parnell's Parliamentary Party who was himself a farmer and he drove as clean a furrow in politics as his ploughshare.

After some years in Clongowes, Kettle came up to University College and it was only a matter of twelve months before he was auditor of the L. & H., reading a paper on *The Celtic Revival*. This was in November 1898, the year that saw the beginning of some sort of representative government in Ireland with the Local Government Act. Yeats had collected his early verse and had written his unfortunately christened *Celtic Twilight*. His *Secret Rose* and *Tables of the Law* were published only a year before along with AE's *Earth Breath;* and *The Countess Cathleen* had been published but not yet staged. Symbol-charioted, our poets had not moved far from their remote, esoteric springs. Kettle was then eighteen years old and this auditorial address provides a convenient yardstick to measure the standards of his University College at an undergraduate level.

The title of the paper—*The Celtic Revival*—should not mislead. It was deliberately significant and did not point only, as it now most commonly does, to a purely literary or linguistic revival. The Celtic revival meant two things to Kettle, as Father Delany, agreeing with him, said on that night: it meant the revival of Celtic literature but much more the revival of the Celt. The young speaker makes it plain that he is not blind to the excellence of the new poets and seers. He pays tribute to its new strange music, to the absence from the new literature of racial hatred and bitter memories and to its generous reception in another capital city, tired of the blatant literature of imperialism. But having paid this tribute—in double-faced coinage, if you will, he abruptly turns down literary considerations in favour of that to which he claims art should be subordinate: the enrichment and betterment of life and, more narrowly, of Irish life. He would expect our men of letters to be chartered in a regenerative movement but thinks that the literary revival shows no confidence in kin and tells its message not to men of its own race but to dilettantes in London. He finds it 'groping in the dust and shrouds of the past not for the lost thread of the labyrinth but for the sorry tinsel of folklore and legend to dress them up for the stranger'. He finds in this 'retrospective, speculative exclusive renaissance' (I repeat his words), 'no manly vigour, no spring of action, no fruit but Dead Sea fruit'.

I interrupt myself to say two things. First, that Kettle was reading Georges Guyau and is here beginning to preach his life-long gospel of art for life's sake, seeking in it the springs of action and life's enrichment; and secondly to draw attention to one who was probably present in his audience. Joyce had entered University College in 1898. He must either have been present or have read this address and, with essential differences in their conclusions, we may note a similar initial critical outlook and very similar language when Joyce approaches the literary side of Kettle's theme. I think this is evident to the reader of Joyce's paper on Mangan, read to the L. & H. in 1902, and his adroitly disparaging review of Lady Gregory's *Poets and Dreamers* in 1903. The shrouds of the past and the tinsel of folklore are their common targets and glimmer through Joyce as through Kettle though each looks for a different mode of redemption. Joyce points to an aesthetic Messiah: Kettle wants action. The Celtic revival in 1898 means for him the revival of the Celt and should have as its fulcrum the Gaelic League, a new University and the new Local Government Act—the latter securing as it did the entrance of the people into Irish administration. This meant eventually the exit of the British garrison.

This undergraduate, coming from the core of Irish life and now trailing his coat for the benefit of late speakers, underestimated the range and indeed the nationalism of Yeats and the not yet so evident nationalism of AE. But it was 1898 and their centres appeared to be still in literary cenacles. What is truly characteristic is Kettle's refusal to isolate literature from life at the bidding of aesthete or seer. He looked to the present and future. The verses he was beginning to write in that year would 'press to touch the throng' and turned away from 'waste lands sown with rancour and fields where we gather but cockle harvests and vain words'.

He followed the philosophy course in college and then spent a year at Innsbruck for health's sake as well as study. At Innsbruck University he read history as well as philosophy under a formidable team of Teutonic professors: Hurter, whose text books are read in our seminaries, 'a man' he wrote of as 'physically noteless, crouching at his desk, cleaving right from wrong, with the sword of justice'; Denifle, that *grosser Tiroler* who put Luther in his place; Pastor, the historian of the Papacy, and that other historian, the leonine Michael whom a later student described to me as looking on his rostrum like Hindenburg on a gun-carriage. Austria presented also for his study its federal problem, eight language questions, the violent beginnings of Pan-Teutonism and it added to these vertical racial divisions the *Los von Rom* religious cross-section. In Innsbruck, furthermore, there was another university question more high-pressured than at home, and as prickly. Philosophy and history were accordingly not class-room fodder only. From academic mangers it overflowed into the streets. It fed such furious riots between German and Italian-speaking students as forced the senate to close the university, bringing Kettle's lectures to a close. History, even Irish history, was a living force about him. He had found in Tyrol more than one memory of the Irish Brigade; the Wild Geese had used beak and claws at Pontlatz Bridge, Prutz and Bozen. But Clio dropped a feather closer at hand. One day, Kettle saw rival demonstrators coming to blows when they had failed to out-sing each other with *Die Wacht am Rhein* and the Garibaldian hymn. The Germans forced their enemy to take refuge in the Café Flunger and beat in vain against the doors barred against them. Thwarted they marched away shouting 'boycottiert Flunger! Boycottiert Flunger!' The Land Leaguer's son felt that his family had given a new word to the German language.

By this time he was reading in many languages and had trenched many fields—philosophy, sociology, history, law and literature. He was beginning to write prose of marked distinction and verse of more laboured utterance. He struggled with an embarrassment of riches and an inevitable sense of indirection. The contrary pull of law, literature and politics is not uncommonly felt by law students and others will have seen note-books like his where the beginning of essays, pungent phrases, fragments of verse under revision, incipient ideas for a historical novel lay cheek by jowl with *Coggs* v *Barnard* and digests of other leading cases. To this sense of indirection there was joined a deep-seated *Welt-schmerz* that went beyond the ordinary world-weariness of the studious adolescent. His mind had not the settled, philosophic cast of John Marcus O'Sullivan's but having come under Hegel's influence he was impatient of what was obviously fragmentary. This passion for the comprehensive, his hunger to reconcile opposites, was innate in him and grew with his appreciation of the Hegelian dialectic and Hegel's conception of history. It did not contribute to his peace of mind. Though in the end, as Shelley says, the understanding grows brighter by gazing on many truths yet light comes painfully and heart and mind suffer in passing away from naive perception. In a paper of 1905, Kettle quoted a passage from Georges Guyau—he was fond of quoting Guyau: 'It is the brain that suffers, it is the brain that throbs with the torment of the unknown, it is the brain that is signed with the sacred wound of the Ideal, it is the brain that quivers under the beak of the winged and ravening intellect'. The quotation had enough of himself in it to be recognized by his friends in the Cui Bono, however much the cloud under which he moved was, stabbed with wit and the warmest humanity. At this date too, as was the fashion, he was reading Schopenhauer, Hegel's passionate opposite number, drawn to him as much by Schopenhauer's escape into art as by his own melancholy moods. Hegel was, however, much more in line with his character. There was much in him that corresponded with what Caird finds most striking in personality: the combination of a deeply idealistic, poetical and religious view of the world with that practical good sense and critical keenness of understanding which are usually the possession of another order of minds.

He was called to the Bar in 1905 but before then his attention focused on contemporary affairs and he became more and more a publicist. He never joined Sinn Féin and one remembers his acute but not unfriendly analysis of its foundation piece—Arthur

Griffith's *Resurrection of Hungary*. He read it to the Cui Bono in 1904 and published it in the same year in *The New Ireland Review*. All the time his charm and his gift for friendship was extending his circle of acquaintance far beyond academic groups. More and more in the Cui Bono he deplored our over-plus of critical intelligence and our dearth of creative effort just as he concealed with difficulty his discontent with the dreams and detachment of the early literary movement. Whilst aware of its worth he wanted a fuller realization of the Irish *comédie humaine* and it was in this expectancy he built his friendship and admiration for Padraic Colum who first introduced the peasant tension to our new stage. His letters to me at this period carried one cry always—'We must humanize ourselves'. He himself was now coming into closest touch with every condition of Irishmen: County Dublin market-gardeners and cattlemen, economists like Father Tom Finlay and T. P. Gill, track-runners and footballers, newspaper men, poets and writers, manual workers, labour leaders and politicians and county councillors. All these people, unknown to each other, had the same story to tell, not of a mere hail-fellow-well-met, but of unforced identity and comradeship. He spoke everyone's language without forsaking his own. All doors were open to him and he subjugated any chance company, not by his exceptional wit merely, but by fellowship.

In public his oratical gift had become manifest. His experience of men and books gave quick reinforcement to a natural gift and his wit had a weight behind it that gave great driving power to his epigrams. Whether on the platform or in his ordinary talk he loved the generalization, the image and the epigram—the badge of the philosopher, the poet and the wit. Sown like Burke's or Grattan's with 'proverbs of freedom' fresh-minted, his public speech, for all its wide sweep, never lost the common touch but swiftly came back with some trenchant phrase that clinched or demolished an argument. The phrase was commonly genial, slamming a cupboard door as Tacitus might have slammed it but opening a window upon a sudden brightness. The introduction to his *Irish Orators,* a characteristic piece of writing too familiar, I hope, for quotation, is a record both of what he admired and of what he practised. It remains a fragment of self-identification. Loving the epigrammatic summing-up, he defends it as one of the rhetorical crafts. He would deny to no speaker 'the wide and deep-shadowed view of traversed altitudes that breaks on the vision of a climber who after long effort had reached the mountain top'. He exulted in such wide prospects. They became his natural climate in speech and writing, happiest when generalization and epigram sparked into image. Admirable also and very characteristic in every respect is Shane Leslie's account of a wayside election meeting in East Tyrone when Kettle was successfully fighting his first parliamentary election. The mountain people came down to meet Kettle and Leslie with fifes playing and blazing torches. Kettle said: 'Friends, you have met us with God's two best gifts to man—fire and music'. His quick response was typical of the warm glow of his speech and his sense of kinship with people.

His student days, with which I am chiefly concerned, were now ended. They had a symbolic close when, to the music of barrel-organs in a student demonstration against a mistaken if not illegal exercise of senatorial authority, he burnt the parchment diploma of his degree on the steps of the Royal University. I am over-running my narrative in touching on his later career and matters of public record. When he was still a law student he had busied himself with politics in north County Dublin and in the city. In 1904 he was the first president of the active Young Ireland Branch of the United Irish League. In that year he was invited by Redmond and John Dillon to accept nomination to fill a parliamentary vacancy in North Kildare. In the event he did not go forward for this uncontested seat but, another invitation being extended in 1906, he fought the brilliant campaign I have mentioned, in East Tyrone, and he held that seat with an increased majority at the general election of 1910.

Growing hardened to public life, he retained on the political platform much of the manner and magnetism of his private address. With head bent forward and slightly rocking frame, dark eyes glowing and very mobile lips, he spoke without gesture and he held his audience in winning intimacy by the familiarity of his drawling speech, leaning effectively in its deeper tones on the unexpected turns of phrase. The effective work of his few years at Westminster was in connection with the Irish Universities Act of 1908.

In the autumn of 1910 he retired from Parliament to take up the professorship of National Economics in the new University. If his college lectures to an able handful of students were informal and casually topical, as I have no doubt they were, I have equally no doubt they were alive and provocative. He might have been happier in a modern literature faculty, but economics was a vital study; the slice of life he handled would bleed with human actuality.

The phrase is his and it sticks in my mind by reason of an evening at the Cui Bono in 1913. Dublin was then convulsed in the labour struggle with the bitter lock-outs of those Larkin years. Our professor of National Economics was late in appearing at our meeting. When he did appear it was with his head bound up with bloodstained bandages and Willie Dawson looked at him and said: 'I see you have been fomenting peace'. As chairman of the Mansion House Peace Committee, Kettle had been as usual at his Hegelian game of reconciling opposites. He had passed into the acted dialectic of history. His position in economics is outlined in two papers written in 1912. Neither is yet wholly outdated but still less a third, written in 1913 in the full impact of the Dublin labour struggle when all his human sympathies were outraged by the rigid inhumanity of the federated employers. That *année terrible* has nowhere been more acutely psycho-analysed than in this paper on *Labour and Civilization*. There is, on the other hand, more fervour than insight in his other contemporary estimate, set out in his *Ways of War*, of the situation which led him, torn by conflicting loyalties, to his gallant lamented death at Ginchy in 1916. Since I am here writing of the student I knew, it is unnecessary as it would also be inept to enter on these issues concerning which he has left his own full apologia. I prefer to continue to think back to earlier years when his talk at the Cui Bono and his reading list disclosed the drift of his mind and the seeds of his action.